One's Company

Christmas 2000

For Tom --

May you come to enjoy increasing delight in your own company, for I can attest that your company can indeed be delightful.

Blessings upon you this Christmastide & always.

Love,
Lisa

One's Company

Reflections on Living Alone

Barbara Holland

A COMMON READER EDITION

THE AKADINE PRESS

One's Company

ISBN 1-888173-08-4

5   7   9   10   8   6

To all my good friends

Contents

Preface

This book was not so much written as accumulated, over a period of eight or nine years, in notes and stray observations that kept piling up. We who make our homes alone find our opinions lie heavy on our hands, with no one around to pass them on to, and can only get rid of them by writing them down. These random thoughts were boxed and moved from place to place, until they began to present a housekeeping problem and it seemed tidiest to make them into a book.

This accumulation process accounts for the various moods and outlooks, the flashes of bossiness as I try to shake some sense into myself, the fits of gloom and flares of wild optimism, the scene changes.

During these years, I lived in three city apartments, a small town, a farmhouse shared with a friend, and, briefly, a house in the suburbs. From time to time one or two of my children would move in with me, and presently move out again. Then I inherited a cottage in the Blue Ridge Mountains, west of Washington, D.C., where I am at the moment. Next year I may be somewhere else. We solitaries are a footloose lot.

In the summer, friends and relations come to visit; in the winter, a lone bear prowls the premises occasionally, the deer grow so brazen they try to get into the kitchen, and the owls call at midday. Even with the leaves off the trees, I can't see my neighbor's chimney smoke. I can barely hear his chain saw.

When I first came to this place the silence was appalling. When guests waved good-bye and drove away, I wanted to race through the dust trail after their cars crying, "Come back! Take me with you!" I'm used to it now, though, and leave my doors open on summer nights and my car keys dangling from the ignition.

I am indebted to all my good friends, from whose company and conversation so much of this has grown. And I am particularly grateful to my brother Andrew, who showed me how to change locks and fuses, and has always come to my rescue when the mechanics of householding are more than I can handle.

Bluemont, Virginia
1992

One's Company

Chapter 1

Here We Are

O Solitude! Where are the charms
That sages have seen in thy face?
—WILLIAM COWPER

Here we are, all by ourselves. All twenty-two million of us, by recent count, alone in our rooms, some of us liking it that way and some of us not. Some divorced, some widowed, some never yet committed.

If we're young and attractive and urban, the magazines call us "singles." Singles are said to live in a joyful flurry of other singles, racing each other through the surf, rising on the corporate ladder, and waking up in the penthouses of singles of the other sex. The darlings of a consumer society, we spend our incomes not on mortgages and disposable diapers but on electronic entertainment, clothes, and exciting cars. Singles rejoice in their freedom up until quite an advanced age, or so they keep telling us, the women until their childbearing years start narrowing down and the men often forever—only five percent of the bachelors over forty will ever marry.

Still, even the busiest of these merrymakers have moments, small but ominous cracks and leaks in the good life; evenings in June when the late sun slants into the apartment and the silence ticks like a bomb; Saturdays in October when the wind creaks down the street and the light chills and sharpens and the skin prickles restlessly.

Others are alone but not single, just solitary. They're too old or too shy or too poor to be singles, or they were recently members of families and are still unadjusted and confused, or they live in the wrong sort of place. They buy a half-loaf of bread and a can of tuna and let themselves into their apartments at the end of the day calling wistfully for the cat, check the unblinking light on the answering machine and sit down to read through the junk mail, absorbing messages about carpet sales and grocery coupons sent in from the great busy world.

There are crazies among us too, women with seventeen parrots and thin old men mumbling to themselves on the bus. People we have met by accident camp out in lofts or deserted offices and come to our house to shower and wash their hair, bringing a whiff of life's precariousness. Without the ballast of families, lone acquaintances ring our doorbell at four in the morning to tell us they've just seen God or Elvis Presley, or they've invented a petroleum substitute or written a poem or had a strange dream. No one was home to tell them to shut up and go back to sleep, so the strange dream took root and grew.

Samuel Johnson, the eighteenth-century curmudgeon and author, said, "The solitary mortal is certainly luxurious, probably superstitious, and possibly mad."

The anarchy of life alone, sometimes called freedom, threatens us with chaos. Fear of chaos can lead to rigidity and tidiness and the multiplication of lists, schedules, and routines, since we have no one but ourselves to bind our lives together. We keep checking ourselves for signs of disintegration: it's important to stay, at the very least, sane.

In more primitive societies all over the world, nobody lives alone, and families accrete in generational layers to the toppling point. There are villages where people may know solitude for only a few hours or days in a lifetime, maybe in a hut on the outskirts, as part of a maturity ritual; the rest of their lives they sleep ears-to-heels with all their relations and apparently like it that way.

Loneliness is peculiarly prevalent in America, built into our foundations somehow, maybe an outgrowth of our newness here and our mixed origins. In older places the citizens draw a kind of membership from nationality and ethnic heritage, and say "I'm French" or "I'm a Serb" with an obvious sense of belonging to an extended family, but we seem to have left this consolation behind when we immigrated. We lost the sense of being fastened to a community instead of free-falling through a void, and a community was a firmer anchor than even the most loyal group of friends.

Loneliness may be a sort of national disease here, and certainly it's a shameful one, more embarrassing to admit than any of the deadly sins. Happy-ever-after has rejected us. The fairy story spit us out as unworthy, and sometimes we suppose perhaps we are.

On the other hand, to be alone but not lonely, alone on purpose, having rejected company rather than been cast out by it, is the American hallmark of a hero. The lone hunter, explorer, cowboy, needing no one; Thoreau, snug and smug in his cabin, his back deliberately turned to the town; now, that's character for you.

This leaves us in a double bind. Here we are, alone because nobody wants us, and lonely because we're so spineless and empty-headed we can't find inspiration in our solitude.

Inspiration in solitude is a major commodity for poets and philosophers. They're all for it. They all speak highly of themselves for seeking it out, at least for an hour or even two before they hurry home for tea.

Consider Dorothy Wordsworth, for instance, wrapping the muffler around her brother's neck, finding his notebook and pencil for him, and waving as he sets forth to look at daffodils all by himself. "How gracious, how benign, is solitude," he said, rudely.

Watch Shakespeare detaching himself from his jolly players and going out for an afternoon to find "sermons in stones and books in the running brooks." Or Tennyson, trotting off to the beach and standing there wondering if it might come on to rain while he jots down, "Break, break, break on thy cold gray stones, O sea," before he hustles home to tell his admiring friends about his experience.

No doubt about it, solitude is improved by being voluntary.

Look at Milton's daughters arranging his cushions and shawls before they tiptoe off, so he can mutter, "And Wisdom's self / Oft seeks to sweet retired solitude / Where, with her best nurse Contemplation, / She plumes her feathers and lets grow her wings." Then he calls the girls to come back and write it down while he dictates.

Byron said, "There is a rapture on the lonely shore, / There is society, where none intrudes," but when you consider Byron's hectic love life, he probably wasn't standing on the beach ten minutes. His schedule was tight. I'm not even sure he ever set foot on a lonely shore. Maybe someone told him about it.

You will have noticed that most of these rapturous types went outdoors to be alone. The indoors was full of loved ones keeping the kettle warm till they came home.

All these high-minded beach-trotters love to make us feel bad about needing company. Sir Philip Sidney, the sixteenth-century poet, sniffed, "They are never alone that are accompanied by noble thoughts," and I guess that puts us in our place. Not only has everyone gone away and left us, but our very thoughts are inadequate. Our thoughts are about whether to call the O'Connors or are they sick and tired of being supportive, and should we eat eggs again or gird up our loins and go out for a sandwich. These are not the thoughts that inspire. And then the mind wanders, and we ask ourselves just what Sir Philip's thoughts were. What *are* noble thoughts, and how do you have them? What are they about? Politics, nature, religion, business ethics? Or are they maybe not thoughts at all but just a vague, self-satisfied *feeling* of nobility, afloat with images of the hereafter and the ocean's roar? And how long can we keep this up, alone in a room?

Forever, if we had any character at all, according to the British psychiatrist Anthony Storr. In *Solitude, A Return to the Self*, Storr, who happens to be married, speaks highly of living alone and says it's essential for serious thinking. Descartes, Newton, Locke, Pascal, Spinoza, Kant, Leibniz, Schopenhauer, Nietzsche, Kierkegaard, and Wittgenstein, he says, were all primarily solitary men, and just look at the mountains of philosophy they churned out. (He seems to think this should make us feel better, and I'm sure it should. I'm working on it.)

The American high priest of solitude was Thoreau. We admire him, not for his self-reliance and his conceited musings, but because he was all by himself out there at Walden Pond, and he *wanted* to be. All alone in the *woods*.

Actually, he lived a mile, or twenty minutes' walk, from his nearest neighbor; half a mile from the railroad; three hundred yards from a busy highway. He had streams of company in and out of the hut all day, asking him how he could possibly be so noble. Apparently the main point of his nobility was that he had neither wife nor servants, and washed his own dish. I don't know who did his laundry; he doesn't say, but he certainly doesn't mention doing his own, either.

Listen to him: "I find it wholesome to be alone the

greater part of the time. To be in company, even with the best, is soon wearisome and dissipating. I love to be alone. I never found the companion that was so companionable as solitude."

Thoreau had his own self-importance for company. Thoreau alone with Thoreau was a crowd. Perhaps there's a message here. The larger the ego, the less the need for other egos around. The more modest, humble, and self-effacing we feel, the more we suffer from solitude, feeling ourselves inadequate company.

Storr suggests that the ability to be happy alone comes from knowing, as a small child, that Mother would be there whenever we needed her. Since mothers have always had other places they needed to be, even if just asleep in bed, this may leave out most of us.

The only woman of record who spoke well of solitude was Greta Garbo. I don't count Emily Dickinson; all she had to do was unlock her bedroom door and go downstairs. She's one of the voluntaries, like Wordsworth out for a walk. She had a family; she just preferred to lurk upstairs. We don't need to. There's nobody in our living room to escape from.

If you live with other people, their temporary absence can be refreshing. Solitude will end on Thursday, or next month when the children come home from camp, and in the meantime you can stretch out your soul until it fills up the whole room, and squander your freedom, coming and going as you please without apology, staying up late to read, eating only when you're hungry, moving at your own pace. The absent will be back. Their winter clothes are in the cedar closet and their dog keeps watching for them from the window; you can tell they'll be back.

When you live alone, the temporary absence of your friends and acquaintances leaves a black hole: *they* may never come back. They've left nothing behind; perhaps they never existed at all. Perhaps you dreamed them. Perhaps they've moved to Seattle.

Those who have lived alone since college days have adjusted imperceptibly over time, but the freshly divorced or widowed are shocked by the silence. Men feel utterly abandoned and desolated at having to wash their own clothes. Women can lose the very sense of their selves, which leaves the room empty indeed.

For ages past, women were defined only in relation to other people, and the definition lingers; a woman may be called a wife and mother for most of her life, while a man is called a husband and father only at his funeral. Even today a solitary woman may feel like the tree falling in the empty forest; alone in a room, nobody's daughter, wife, lover, mother, or executive assistant, her ectoplasm thins out until the furniture shows through. Let someone else walk in and she solidifies in relation to the visitor, but alone her outlines fade.

Psychologist John Bradshaw, in *Bradshaw On: The Family*, says, "We cannot have an identity all alone. Our reality is shaped from the beginning by a *relationship*."

Solitude strikes hardest at those who are suddenly alone after a death or divorce or the departure of children. We may waste long hours of our new freedom just sitting there, hands folded patiently, waiting for someone to need us, someone to say "When's dinner?" or "Where's my math book?" so we can return to our skins and be us again.

The Chinese have a ritual for calling your spirit back to you when it drifts away, in madness or nightmares; they recite a litany of all your ancestors and relatives, place-names and former street addresses, as landmarks so your wandering spirit can find you again. Alone, with no one to remind her of her self, a woman's spirit can detach itself and float loose, producing a weird sense of third-personness. With no one to watch us, we start watching ourselves, from a slight distance, like a woman in a movie, so as not to disappear. This separation from self feels like a kind of madness, and probably is: all over the country, women peering closely at themselves as they feed the cat.

Meanwhile, recently divorced, widowed, or abandoned men are walking back and forth on the sidewalk in front of their homes. Sitting on porches and in bars and movie theaters and on the front steps. Without another person they can neither concentrate nor sleep, and no one tells them they're wearing one black sock and one Argyle. No one reminds them to turn the clock ahead in April, and their refrigerator holds nothing but a withered half a lemon.

Most men find it hard to work up a meaningful relationship with an empty room, and a room with nobody else in it is empty, no matter how much furniture a girl-friend has helped them buy and arrange. One man I know, abandoned by his wife, keeps toothbrushes. He keeps the fresh, boxed-and-wrapped toothbrush in the medicine cabinet, of course, because he read an article recommending it in case some lovely young thing decides to sleep over, but he also keeps a plastic cup full of un-wrapped, used-looking toothbrushes on the windowsill. They represent a houseful of loving family, and cheer him slightly, briefly, when he sees them in the morning: a single toothbrush can be a terrible sight.

Men find it sadder to take care of themselves, laundry depresses them, and they feel peculiarly trapped by their dwellings. You meet them wandering, and they say, "My apartment was driving me crazy," or "I couldn't stand the empty house," as if the very walls had turned savage. For a man who has had a family and lost it, home seems an unnatural place to be. He may make gastronomical delights for his friends, but alone he drinks instant coffee at dawn and by night, eats Chinese take-out from the carton, watching television.

He stays out later and later, postponing the dry click of the latchkey. He uses the phone in the bar to call a dozen people he doesn't really want to see. He looks in the phone book for people he knew in college. In high school. He goes back to his wife, or even back to his mother. Or, of course, he marries again, an easier, swifter cure for men than for women.

For a woman, at first the condition seems temporary—surely the door will open, and someone walk in, and life become magically normal any minute now. Then it begins to stretch out and feel, if not permanent, at least longer. As long as an apartment lease, or even two. Adjustments must be made.

It's inconvenient, this solitary life. Nobody lends a hand. We can't say, "Would you get the door for me? —hand me the towel? —hold up the other end? —go see what's making that funny noise? —grab the cat while I shove the pill down her? —answer the phone? —mail a letter? —put your finger on this knot?" Hanging a picture, we punch a dozen holes in the wall because no one will stand across the room and decide. We do it ourselves or not at all, and when we have clothes to drop off at the cleaners we drive around and around looking for a parking space because there's no one to wait in the car. Only we will carry out the trash and carry in the groceries and cope with the IRS and confirm the plane reservation and open the mayonnaise and take the car to the shop and try to explain to the scornful mechanic about the way it wobbles. If the couch is too heavy for one person to move, it stays where it is, waiting for the next strong guest. And only we will answer when we speak.

The condition of loneliness ebbs and flows, influenced by body chemistry and the weather, but needing to talk goes on forever. It's more basic than needing to listen. Oh, we all have friends we can tell important things to, people we can call to say our daughter got into Harvard or we lost our job or broke our arm. It's the daily small change of complaints and observations and opinions that backs up and chokes us. We can't really call a friend to say we got our feet wet walking home, or it's getting dark earlier now, or we don't trust that new Supreme Court justice.

Some people can, of course. I have a friend who does. She called me last week just to say she'd thought she'd lost her car keys, but then they turned up in the pocket of her coat, the gray coat she hardly ever wears because the shoulders are too tight.

I know how she feels. We all know. Solemn scientific

surveys show that all us solitaries talk at length to our-selves and our pets and the television. We ask the cat whether we should wear the blue suit or the yellow dress, and does it think we'll need an umbrella. There's nothing wrong with this. It's good for us, and a lot less embar-rassing than the woman in front of us in the checkout line who's telling the cashier that her niece Melissa may be coming to visit on Saturday, and Melissa is very fond of hot chocolate with marshmallows, which is why she bought the marshmallows though she never eats them herself.

It's important, as I said, to stay sane.

It's important to stop waiting and settle down and make ourselves comfortable, at least temporarily, in this moonscape, and find some grace and pleasure in our con-dition, not smugly like a British poet but like a patient enchanted princess in a tower, learning to wring honey from a stone.

After all, here we are. It may not be where we ex-pected to be, but for the time being we might as well call it home.

Chapter 2

Lovers

The moon has set, and the Pleiades; it
is midnight, and time passes, and I
sleep alone.

—SAPPHO

It's generally accepted that the first thing needed by people who live alone is a lover, or, failing that, lovers. It's
the one facet of our lives that everyone, particularly long-
married friends of both sexes, takes a keen interest in.
Respectable people with unexceptionable spouses will listen to the details for hours, leaning across the kitchen
table to offer more coffee and advice. If we don't have a
full-time partner, we're expected to put in a good deal of

time and energy looking, because what is life without one? Especially for a woman, it's hardly life at all.

We may be a research chemist with a fascinating job, an apartment people would kill for, and a hundred friends, but everyone knows that these are but dust and ashes without a man. In more romantic times, love, true love, was the point. A woman might have her heart broken at seventeen and spend the rest of her life chastely grieving, admired and respected by all. Now she'd be bundled off to therapy after six months; the emphasis has shifted.

Through many civilized centuries it was taken for granted that women either married or they didn't have any sex life at all. Since marriage was a full-time job and usually involved producing up to a dozen babies, dead or alive, women who wanted to do something else with their years opted for the single life and chastity, mostly in the homes of relatives. Or else they didn't exactly opt out of marriage but just weren't asked, and decided to make the best of it and write novels; being single in a middle-class household with servants left plenty of time on your hands.

Until recently, sex itself wasn't considered a compelling factor for women, or not for nice women; the lower orders were allowed their animal appetites. No one suggested that Jane Austen or Joan of Arc or Louisa May Alcott would be mentally and physically healthier if she hung out in the right sort of bar or answered some Personals ads. For your really decent girl, sex was only the price she paid for a home, a social position, children.

This was turned upside down in the sixties, and sex for the single woman was pronounced to be, first, a basic human right and then, by the seventies, a necessity. "Promiscuous" dropped from the language; instead, we were "sexually active," which sounds as if we hopped around in the sheets like fleas, and it was good for us. Sex put roses in the cheeks and spring in the step and toned up the system and protected us from various illnesses, possibly psychosomatic, and the milder forms of madness. Chastity became a health risk; the unbedded withered emotionally and physically until they dried up and blew away like the husk of a crab claw skittering across the beach. It was a sign of hostility, too; women who slept in this unnatural way, alone, hated the world and should seek professional help.

Love was nice but not necessary. One of the early revelations of feminism was that women were no different from men in these matters and just as well pleased by impersonal sex with partners whose last names they hadn't bothered to learn. Magazines and family doctors and even parents adopted the new views, and whole industries sprang up to service the new national hobby.

It crashed in the eighties. Herpes, the first warning tremor, was followed by the earthquake of AIDS. The new industries and magazines fought valiantly to shore sex up, and articles appeared on the fun of condoms and how they added a whole merry new dimension to fore-play, but the shock had gone too deep and changed the climate. Even the least religious or superstitious among us now feel uneasily that something out there doesn't ap-prove of sex with strangers, and whatever that something is, it has a lot more clout than our mothers. Sex as a sport and pastime has been replaced by exercise. Jogging. "Working out." This may or may not be an improvement; exercise is a solitary, inward-looking concern and lacks the human dimension, even if you run with a friend.

Now that we're no longer encouraged to find a new partner every night, we're expected to set up what they call a relationship; select a mate and go together, holding hands, to be tested for AIDS; and vow to sleep with no other for the duration of the agreement, for hygienic rather than emotional reasons. This constitutes a commitment, as they say. It spreads a certain solemnity over the bed-ding. The shared test for HIV has taken on some of the weight that once hung on the diamond engagement ring or, more recently, the joint apartment lease.

Men, the women say, fight shy of commitment. Or perhaps there simply are no men any more.

The complaints ring out from kitchen tables across the land, especially in eastern cities. There are no men.

They're all either married or gay. Men over forty are only interested in women under thirty. Women over forty can only hope for men past eighty and bedridden. *Why* aren't there any men? Where did they *go*?

You hear it even from pretty women in their twenties, with cheerful hearts and good jobs. You see them going out with monsters.

Always before in times of war or mass emigration the young men went away and didn't come back, and the women they would have married slept alone, but that doesn't explain the current problem.

Before the revolutions of the sixties many homosexual men compromised and married, for social or family reasons. Now they're free to follow their own road, taking a chunk of the population out of the running, though not as large a chunk as it seems in some cities and some lines of work. Certainly they don't help the statistics, but they aren't the whole cause of the shortage.

One major factor seems to be an increase in deliberate bachelors. According to the record, in 1970 only 9.4 percent of men aged thirty to thirty-four had never married; in 1987 the figure jumped to 23 percent. Between 1980 and 1989, the number of men between thirty-five and forty-four who had never married more than doubled, to outnumber the women in their age group by half a million.

(We're looking at formal, legal marriages, of course; they probably had various long-term domestic relationships that never got to the altar.)

Back in the glory days of the women's movement, feminism was supposed to benefit men too. Men, once they got used to the idea, would rejoice to have strong, confident, independent women by their sides, and they'd be released from the armor-plate of machismo, let their hair down, and turn over half the financial burdens to their wives with glad relief. Some did. Some took the whole movement as hostility and are still nursing resentment. Things just aren't the same between the sexes. Along with the old inequities, we lost a certain sweetness between us.

From a man's-eye view, marriage has suffered. It may be that for every man who wants an equal companion in an equally shared life, six only wanted uncritical admiration and a home arranged for their comfort, and who can blame them? It sounds like heaven. If you'd been raised to believe this was your birthright, wouldn't you howl at losing it?

Nobody wants to admit it, but even in the good old days not everyone married for reasons of passionate love. Women married for security, and because the alternatives were nasty, and men married to be taken care of, to be the center of someone's exclusive attention, to own a kingdom where their word was law and meals were served as soon as they were hungry.

Now they're expected to cook, or at least arrange for, some of the meals themselves, and to come home not to a well-chilled martini but to a basket of laundry. It doesn't have the same allure.

Many new fathers nowadays take a kindly interest in even very young children, which is charming and good for everyone, but nobody wants to clean house. Recent surveys show that the more housework a man does the less happy he rates his marriage, and the less the more. (Surveys also show that men think they do nearly three times as much housework as they actually do.)

In more puritanical days, regular sex was a reason for a man to set up housekeeping with a woman, but now sex is only a phone call away and volunteers are plentiful; the more attractive single men I know hardly bother to pick up the phone until it rings.

A bachelor with a smoldering resentment of independent-minded women, a reliable housecleaning service, and a friendly neighborhood restaurant just doesn't find romantic commitment that urgent a matter, or not yet, anyway. Not now. Later.

I do know a scattering of heterosexual bachelors who complain that they never meet any nice women. One and all they're shy, modest, and socially inept. They can't walk up to a woman and start a conversation, and their palms sweat when they have to dance. They spend a lot of time in their apartments, wondering where all the women are. In other times and cultures the family and the social web would have found them their girls, but we're all on our own here.

The only way to meet these men is to get a job as a waitress in the diner where they eat every night. They wipe their cutlery absentmindedly on the napkin and open a book: drop a tray of dishes on the floor beside them to get their attention.

They're dreadfully poor, though. In America shy people never get rich.

Younger women have better luck and wider choices. It stands to reason that the men most happily formed by temperament and inclination for good marriages marry early and stay married, thinning the ranks of the available.

Those of us recently divorced from a man who ran off with a girl named Bambi may be so ripe and bursting with rage that the main reason we want to meet a man is to spit in his eye. Those recently widowed after happy days, when they recover, may set forth in all brave innocence to find another fine fellow, and sometimes even do, since people often find what they expect to find.

All single women are urged to make the effort to locate a long-term man, almost any man, with the possible exception of the married. Affairs with married men are frowned on by most major religions, and even among the irreligious they aren't considered sporting. Secrecy is only sometimes fun. In our youth there may have been a certain dizzy illicit thrill in secret affairs with boys our parents disapproved of; we knew our parents were wrong about them, and if they found out we could have a grand old righteous row. It's harder to convince ourselves it's righteous to take up with someone else's husband, no matter how unhappy he says they are together. Of course, this is strictly between you and your conscience, but on the practical side, you wind up playing solitaire on Christmas Eve and wondering what to do with your summer vacation. A man with a family spends time with his family, leaving you miserable in several ways at once; the combination of guilt and jealousy is so uncomfortable it's worth taking pains to avoid.

Besides, statistics show that the stinkers rarely do leave their wives as promised, and if they do they often repent and go back.

The other day America's favorite advice columnist printed a letter from a widow in her fifties complaining that, since her husband died, all their old friends had dropped her, she was lonely, she had no one to go to the movies with. The answer was brisk: she was to quit sulking and give a party, perhaps hot dogs and baked beans on a Sunday, with football on the television, and "don't fail to include three or four extra men." O happy Ann Landers, in her magical world where three or four unattached men, presumably solvent and heterosexual and of suitable age, sit by the phone longing to spend Sunday eating baked beans with a widow in her fifties!

The questing women are told to lower their standards because they're expecting too much in a man. The invented, projected lover always looks good, and why not? Without a resident male we're free to invent one, and why bother to invent a toad? Relationships, like Easter eggs, look better from the outside, and the one we see through the mists is a beauty, all consoling hugs and laughter and handfasted walks in the autumn woods.

Reality has rougher edges. The nineteenth-century explorer and mystic Alexandra David-Néel wrote to her husband, "It is only in dreams that human beings are sweet and so good to have near us . . . in reality they are the sharp stones in the corners that we hit against and are wounded by." (Actually her husband seems to have been a pussycat. Once she went off on a journey and didn't come back for fourteen years. He waited.)

We're told to stop dreaming and take whatever we can find, and probably if we lower our standards far enough we'll find some sort of man to share our lives, at least for a while; princes are thin on the ground but there are toads a-plenty. In *Pride and Prejudice* Elizabeth Bennet's friend Charlotte, a woman of sense and spirit, marries the appallingly awful Mr. Collins, conceited and pompous and boot-licking and condescending and long-winded, with nothing to recommend him but a comfortable house. Charlotte doesn't seem to regret it. In 1813 her options weren't extensive, but even today, with jobs and apartments there for the taking, women can bend their lives into strange shapes in return for male company.

We want to be part of a couple. Uncoupled, we are all slightly diminished in sheer bulk, and a woman more so than a man; we simply don't tip the scales, in any situation, as solidly as a couple does, or command the same respect, or take up as much space when we walk into a roomful of people. Though never as small as half a couple, we're usually, depending on personality, only about two thirds of one. There's a danger, in certain moods and at certain times of year, of simply blowing off the face of the world like a scrap of crumbled paper.

So we take what we can get. A recent phenomenon is the long-term unmarried arrangement, the census bureau's "Person of Opposite Sex Sharing Living Quarters," or POSSLQ. Quite often these drift on and on without reaching any particular destination and then dissolve, and we divide the books and videotapes and pack them into our separate cartons and say good-bye, and there we are alone again and several years older, after time that feels wasted, as if permanent coupling had been the only point of those years and we'd missed it.

Closing the sale, as they say in the used-car business, has grown elusive. Sometimes it seems to be more a co-incidence of timing than a sudden flare-up of committed passion; suddenly the moment ripens and falls from the tree. With women this often coincides with birthdays and the biological timetable; if there are going to be children they will have to come soon. Men have no deadlines for children but they aren't immune to birthdays either. *It's time*, they think, as if a beeper had gone off in their pock-ets. Sometimes one marriage in a group of friends will do it; sometimes an unrelated incident triggers the mo-ment—a burglary, a car accident, a death in the family, something that pulls back the curtain and exposes the fragility of life, its chanciness, and the presence of sinister forces out there, calling for a permanent second person to reinforce the fort.

Bachelors, when asked, say they haven't yet found the right woman, but the right time is what they mean: the beeper hasn't yet gone off. As soon as it does, even if they have no immediate prospects, they set the wheels in motion and are usually signing papers at City Hall within months. It's a buyer's market.

As for women, cold statistics show that, no matter how low our expectations, some will never marry and some, having been married, won't marry again. By age sixty-five, 41 percent of women live alone. A happy marriage is a great blessing, though, and there's no harm in staying hopeful as long as it doesn't take up too much of our attention. The single-minded search eats into our lives.

If marriage is what we're looking for and we keep coming home without it, then we keep, in our own eyes, failing: failing makes us feel bad. If we're hoping for a man to love us and no man shows up to do so, then we've been rejected by invisible legions of men. Rejection makes us feel unworthy. If we keep our eyes on this distant goal, we miss the scenery and lose the pleasures of the journey. If we keep telling ourselves we really need love and a man, we begin to feel inadequate alone and threatened by strange noises in the night.

A man on the prowl for female companionship can tell himself he's a wolf inspecting the sheep; a woman in search of a man can feel more like the sheep offering herself up to the wolves, a disagreeable position, especially if the wolves don't notice.

We're pummeled with advice on how to conduct the search, from moving to a city where the odds are better to taking a course in automobile mechanics or hanging around in Laundromats offering to help the bachelors roll their socks. We can give up the perfectly swell job where we're surrounded by other women and go find work with a construction company or down a mine. According to the advice-mongers, no boredom or inconvenience should be too grim to tackle. Those of us who consider ourselves intelligent and decently educated and suitably employed may weep with embarrassment, but it's a leveling and humbling condition, this search, where Ph.D. and CEO rub shoulders with the gum-chomping shop clerk, and hunt in the same fields.

Perhaps we should drive around town looking for solitary male drivers in presentable cars and smash into their fenders. Perhaps, over the exchange of insurance cards, love will bloom. It sounds more exciting than Laundromats.

Or we can just get on with the business of living, while remaining open to happy accidents.

A restless, mobile society like ours has its good news and its bad. Men and women alike have lost the social continuity and network that used to provide mates who, if not dazzling, were at least predictable, coming from known backgrounds. On the plus side, we've gained exposure. We move around and meet people, fellow passengers stranded in a blizzard at O'Hare, tenants in the new apartment building, new faces in the office. Poor Charlotte in *Pride and Prejudice* had a static circle of calling acquaintances in rural Hertfordshire, and absent a lucky connection on holiday at Bath or during a London visit, she could assess her future options by the time she was ten. For us, anyone can happen.

We can read all those Personals ads, appearing in ever-growing numbers in local publications. These are written by such attractive and accomplished people, even allowing for pardonable exaggeration, that it seems something basic must have gone wrong with the system. How did people used to meet?

At parties, often. Party giving seems to have changed, and shrunk into the brief space in December when the same faces gather annually and true love seldom walks unexpectedly into the room, locking eyes with you and burrowing through the crowd to your side.

"People have gotten lazy," says my friend Ann. "They're too lazy to give parties any more."

"Too busy," I offer charitably.

"Too selfish."

Too few housebound housewives these days, maybe, frantic for the sight and sound of adults by Saturday night, and with energy and time to spare. Now, after a forty-hour business week with housework in the evenings and errands on weekends, a party is agonizing hard work.

So, confined to the people we already know, we advertise for strangers. "Eclectic, blond, attractive." "Sensual." "Blond bombshell." "Fun-loving." Men over five-foot-ten say how tall they are; under that, they state the maximum height of their future love. Men often mention their weight, too. Size seems to be basic to the male self-image, and the amount of space men displace in the world is their territory, marked off in air. What they want in a woman is beauty, pure and simple, ranging from a modest "pretty but not flashy" or "curvaceously slender" to "extremely beautiful" and "preferably a model or a model type." Education is mentioned rarely and politics never. Some men specify precise measurements of bust and waist, and most have exact age brackets: "21–27," "23–33," "26–31."

Women are looking for men who are sincere, employed, thoughtful, successful, stable, and affectionate. Both sexes, dreaming as they draft their ads, see candlelit dinners, music, travel, walks on the beach. Dream mates float ethereally through the quiet apartments of the advertisers: dream fathers for the women, magazine covers for the men. Happiness by Hollywood.

What everyone's actually groping for, through the artificial mists, is harder to put in an ad; the touch of kindred, the shared current of light. Don Marquis, co-creator with his cockroach of the immortal *archy and mehitabel*, said, "All religion, all life, all art, all expression come down to this: to the effort of the human soul to break through its barriers of loneliness, of intolerable loneliness, and make some contact with another seeking soul." This would sound silly in an ad.

The hidden benefit of the Personals ad is that both of you, writer and respondent, have admitted the shameful secret of loneliness. It's a start, anyway.

After studying the columns for months, I broke down and answered one, to see if it could actually be done.

He and I struggled on the phone with the usual cautious exchange of information (is this person maybe some kind of nut?) and then I suggested we meet somewhere public after work for a drink. He was unable to think of a place, and for some reason so was I, memory struck dumb by confusion, so he picked me up on a street corner.

He looked better than I'd expected. He wasn't fat and he had all his hair. It turned out he didn't drink, though, so as an alternative we went to Chinatown and were tucking into our fried noodles and wonton by twenty after five.

I tried to make light conversation, but he turned it firmly aside. He had some things to ask me. He needed to check my qualifications, and he went down quite a long list of searching questions about my marriage, divorce, job history, psychiatric therapy if any, general health, and so on, rather like an application for a loan. This man was serious. He hadn't sunk all that money into an ad just to sit and chat, or even to roll in the hay; he needed a wife to replace the one who'd left, and he was out looking with commendable determination.

With the shrimp lo mein he said he was sure I had some questions to ask him, and I tried to think what I'd ask if I were interested: his house, his mortgage, his ex-wife, whether kids came with the deal? All I came up with was whether he had any pets.

He had a dog, but it was, he hastened to assure me, very well trained. So well trained that when he put its dinner down on the kitchen floor, the dog would sit there indefinitely, forever if need be, even while my companion left the house, waiting by its dinner for the word, "eat," that gave it permission.

I said I'd never heard anything so sadistic in all my born days, and the evening languished, and broke up early. Height and weight aren't everything. By seven I was hungry again.

Ah well. Shocked as our grandmothers would be, there are indeed all those Personals ads. There are people out there. Just stay in well-lighted public places, remain alert for signs of peculiarity, and make sure any sex is safe. You might even find true love, I suppose, or at least someone sane to go sailing with.

In the meantime, while we're looking, or just waiting,

or trying to ignore the whole matter, there we are alone in bed, with most of us scarcely appreciating the joy of stretching our legs out in any direction and using both pillows at once. The great revolution won us the right to unmarried sex. How come no one will help us exercise it?

The distinguished and crotchety seventeenth-century scholar Robert Burton, a bachelor, considered lust an unfortunate disease, distracting and conducive to melancholy. He offers us some ancient cures for it, most of them even more trouble than finding a mate. Drinking the root of a mandrake is recommended, although the book of simples I'm looking at says mandrake promotes conception, which seems contradictory. The parings from an ass's hoof help too. He doesn't say how you take these, whether you make a tea out of them or just munch them up, or where you buy them if you don't have your own ass.

Quite a few of Burton's sources cite "evacuations and purges . . . and blood-letting above the rest." It stands to reason that when you've been purged to the staggering point and then generously bled, you lose some of your interest in sex. Being run down by a truck would do it too. Further, he says, "Those old Scythians had a trick to cure all appetite of burning lust by letting themselves bleed under the ears, and to make both men and women barren." Birth control the hard way.

He continues, "Here they make medicines to allay lust, such as putting camphor on the parts, and carrying it in the breeches (one saith) keeps the pintle flaccid. A noble virgin being sick with this affliction, a Physician prescribed . . . that she wear on her back for twenty days a thin sheet of lead pierced with many holes; and . . . chew frequently a preparation of coriander, lettuce-seed and vinegar, and so freed her of her malady." Other suggestions include willow-leaf tea, which, if you drink enough, cures you of sex forever. Also "the right stone of a wolf, brayed, and oil or water of roses will cause weariness of venery." "Brayed" means crushed or ground up, and I suppose that's the wolf's right testicle we're working on, and I'm sure this would irritate the wolf and probably the zookeeper as well. Must I do this myself, or may I send my pharmacist instead?

"Dried mint with vinegar in the uterus" will dampen yearnings, as will "Canabis seed." And here you were wondering what to do with all that leftover cannabis seed in the refrigerator.

"Carrying a Verbena herb," Burton assures us, "extinguisheth lust, and pulverized frog, beheaded and dried up." He doesn't say whether you can just carry the dried frog, like the verbena, or need to do something more personal with it. "Anoint the genitals and belly and chest with water in which opium Thebaicum has been dissolved; Camphor is in the highest degree inimical to lust, and dried coriander diminishes coitus and hinders erection . . . Give verbena in a potion, and the pintle will not lift for six days."

So it's not as if we didn't have plenty of remedies.

Even without sex, it's probably a good idea for the genders to stay in touch, meet, play, gossip, and cook in each other's kitchens from time to time. When either goes too long without the other we tend to get peculiar in our separate ways; the natural differences between us grow and accrete, like coral reefs, without the abrasive contact to keep the bristles smoothed down. Intimacy across the gender barrier is hard enough at the best of times—the best of times is about age eighteen, on campus—but after we've been separated from each other too long, when we do meet it's less like the bees and the flowers than like the clang of two suits of armor colliding on the darkling plain.

Men alone may develop a lust for news. They rise early and watch the stuff on television, drive to work listening to it on the radio, then buy a paper and read it on their desks. If there's an evening paper they read that too, after the early news on television and before the late news at eleven, in front of which they sit earnestly absorbing their sixth bulletin on tropical storm Henry, off Bermuda, and a threatened strike of tin-miners in Bolivia. No matter how dull or how ominous, the news pumps through their bloodstreams all day; it's oxygen, nourishment, reality. Finally, when not even the all-news cable channel can wring out another word, when no new message has come from the tin-miners and Henry is moving out to sea, our man detaches his grip and lets himself down into sleep. Sleep, until sunrise brings him his next transfusion.

The impersonality of the news insulates a lonely man from his own life. Disconnect it, and he finds himself a hollow sack of skin crumpling down over his own shoe-tops. It makes him hard to talk to; if you have something to tell him you'll have to get Dan Rather or the *Times* to say it for you.

Presently he may start reading between the lines, shaping his own news. His politics may drift toward the lunatic right, or he may fall into the obsession with conspiracy, an underreported psychiatric disorder. He sees conspiracy in the fall of a leaf or the back of a cabdriver's neck. A flood in Arkansas, a shooting in Nicaragua, and a child falling down a well are linked to each other and to the dark purposes of half a dozen international bankers in Zurich. Without a woman to laugh at him, paranoia stalks the shadowy corridors of his skull.

A woman alone may grow house-proud, fussy and tidy, cherishing her living quarters as if they were family. This used to be the crotchet of the middle-aged, but now it's turning up in younger women, alone in apartments that are no longer casual way stations on the road to marriage, haphazard and fluttering with discarded stockings. Once, a city girl's furniture was pinned together out of canvas and tubing and painted packing boxes; a sneeze would blow it away. It looked, like the girls, alert and weightless, ready to move on. Anything more serious would have meant they'd given up, resigned themselves to the status quo. Now, quite early in life, these same women may buy real furniture, and arrange it and care for it. Choose their own china and bath towels, instead of waiting for the monogrammed wedding presents of the past. They may even iron the sheets. Manless they may be, for the moment, but at least not homeless. Even in high-rise apartments, they make people wipe their feet at the door; they hand you a coaster with your drink and watch to be sure you use it. A visit from a nephew is a day in hell.

They develop habits. While their neighbor, the man, is nursing his international paranoia, they're nursing compulsions, straightening the magazines on the coffee table and disinfecting the spotless sink.

Presently they realize that men ruffle the rugs and

leave damp towels on the bed and shaving cream on the mirror, and they're relieved when the weekend's over and they can set things to rights again. When Prince Charming finally canters in, they make him tie his white horse outside, and stare unnervingly at him as if daring him to move the needlepoint cushion from its accustomed place on the couch. What's he doing here anyway, smelling of horse, when he's already been replaced by tables and chairs?

Life with the opposite sex may have its drawbacks, but it modifies us. It keeps us flexible. Living alone, we need to make a conscious effort to number the other gender, however young or old or unsuitable as lovers, among our friends.

And above all, of course, we need our friends.

Chapter 3

Friends

Only solitary men know the full
joys of friendship. Others have their
families; but to a solitary and an exile
his friends are everything.

—WILLA CATHER

There's a qualitative difference between the friendships of
the married and the unmarried. Couples, strictly speaking, don't really need friends; they have them to break
the monotony and establish their position in the scheme
of things. They have friends who are like themselves:
business associates, neighbors, the parents of children
comparable to their own children. Once or twice a year
they invite them all to a party, and pause for a moment

in the kitchen doorway, holding a tray, and count heads and consider them, thinking "This is us; this is where we fit."

The family itself is a semiprivate organization with a tough skin around it, and the secret life between husband and wife, parents and children, tends to exclude other intimate relationships as a kind of disloyalty, almost adulterous. The social network is the larger tribe, or clan, of similar people that marks off the family's place in the world. Personal affection is almost beside the point.

These matched couples invite each other to dinner, or go out to dinner together, on a weekend night. Orderly as a dance, the Browns and the Jacksons go to dinner at the Joneses', and the following week the Jacksons and the Joneses go to dinner at the Browns'. Dinners are for couples. You can tell: count the chairs that came with the dinner table and divide the number by two.

Those who were never married knew this all along, but for the recently divorced or widowed it comes as a shock. No matter how often you have fed the Joneses, once you're alone you will never eat their dinners again, or at least never on a weekend night, in the dining room. At the kitchen table on a Tuesday, maybe, with the kids squabbling over homework and your friend Mrs. Jones telling you kindly that there's plenty of spaghetti and you might as well stay and eat.

Or you may not even get this far. The Joneses may have decided, after the divorce, that it was simply easier to stay friends with your husband than with you, and feed him instead. For a variety of reasons, single men have more family appeal than single women.

Having an extra man around makes the married woman, who issues most invitations, feel young and attractive. Her husband enjoys the titillating mix of envy and complacency at contrasting his life with his guest's. Both feel mildly responsible for seeing that he's fed; any woman can feed herself, but it's still widely believed, if only half consciously, that a man will starve without a resident woman and is therefore entitled to food from the community. When he walks in, bearing a bottle of wine, he brings a whiff of adventure and freedom to the couple's orderly world. A man alone looks like a free-ranging spirit, bold and unfettered, while a woman alone looks more like a lost lamb bleating for help.

No matter how independent she really is, a single woman can seem like a mine field of potential problems. A married friend unsure of her marriage feels threatened, since everyone knows that any woman alone will do anything to get her hands on any man, including someone else's husband. No husband worries that the bachelor may make off with his wife, because he sees him as fleeing from domestic commitment with his independence clutched to his chest. Besides, as noted, the wife usually issues the invitations, and she would simply rather invite someone to flirt with her than someone to flirt with her husband.

And again, how is this unattended female to get back home after dinner? Will she have come in a car, or must someone drive her home, or go out and find her a taxi, or walk her to her door or her parking lot? Must the host do this, leaving his other guests? Why can't she find an escort of her own? What will she want next, help with her taxes? Her furniture moved, her car started on cold mornings, her plane met? What a bother she is, this solitary female who has to be walked like a dog, and what if she invites us back? Won't it be depressing, just the three of us? Easier not to invite her at all.

The newly single woman will lose married friends, sometimes with brutal abruptness, and the pain of this rejection comes on top of the previous loss and stings like lemon juice in the eye. Sometimes it happens more slowly, and the erstwhile friends still call to chat occasionally and invite her to the big annual party, but can't find a way to fit her into ordinary life. The connection sags and breaks. She has no place in the old orderly arrangements any more. She's unassimilable. As in the song on *Sesame Street*, one of these things is not like the other.

It takes a long time to realize that the loss of familiar

couples isn't all that great, because these are not the friends, these generic social conveniences, that we need now. We need more. We need the kind of friend we had when we were ten or twelve, back when friends meant everything and lovers and husbands were just a smudge on the horizon.

If we're lucky we can salvage some who happen to be married but love us more than social order just the same, and stand by. We can meet them for lunch. Lunch is a sustaining institution; it's time out, free time, without overtones of social and domestic ritual. We ask after their husbands; they ask after our romantic prospects. We ask after their children.

For a couple with children, we may even turn into that useful item, the family friend. This involves taking a fairly intense, steady, alert interest in their offspring, so it's well to like them quite a lot before we embark. We can't fake it, or not for long, and we're going to be spending considerable time with them. The role calls for expensive, carefully chosen birthday presents on the correct day, and trips to the zoo, perhaps even whole weekends that the children spend rollicking in our apartments, or whole vacations we spend feeding and entertaining them while their parents jaunt through Europe. The family friend is invaluable to the couple, and gets routinely invited for those otherwise dreary public holidays like

Christmas, which the family friend attends cheerfully and helpfully, bearing gifts and washing dishes. It's a niche formerly filled by aunts, uncles, and resident grandparents. Sometimes, on bad mornings, it feels like a niche formerly filled by live-in servants and poor relations. Men as well as women are eligible. Some are temperamentally better suited for it than others, and for these it has its advantages—a shadow home, guaranteed company, a reservoir of potential kindness stored up against our hour of need.

Remember, though, that there's always the underlying whisper of exclusion: we are not quite one of them. We're said to be just like family, but we aren't, not really. We're not even among the first to be called in times of death or marriage. They may not circle the wagons and leave us outside to be scalped, but they will certainly go off for a weekend and leave us behind.

We don't need to have been widowed or divorced to lose friends to marriage, of course. We can live merrily single with a circle of friends of both sexes, all of us in and out of each other's apartments for years, sharing a house at the shore and feeding each other's cats at vacation time, and then suddenly the others all become parts of couples, like the finale of a Gilbert and Sullivan operetta. The wind in our face is the breath of their doors closing, one by one.

Single friends are better for us, because they need us in the same way and for the same things that we need them, and they're ready for a weekend drive to an upstate flea market, or to sit up all night talking, but they're unstable. It comes with the territory. Having no reason to be here rather than somewhere else, they go somewhere else. They move to Vail for the skiing or to Key West for the fishing; they take jobs on the opposite coast; they fall in love and vanish. Every year they send Christmas cards saying the same thing, how we must get together in the coming year, how it's been too long; maybe we can meet in New York for dinner, or you could come and stay if you don't mind the couch, now that little Gabriel's in the guest room. Then, at some unnoticed point, the cards stop coming.

You can lose friends one by one, replacing them as you go along, or you can lose the whole network within a few months.

There will be the year—there always is the year—when you buy a bottle of really decent champagne in December, because someone worthy of it will surely drop by, and it stays in the refrigerator till March, when you sit down and drink the whole thing yourself and burst into tears.

At certain seasons in a person's life, new friends arrive

effortlessly. Open the door and charming strangers walk in, make themselves at home, and become friends. If we and they lead fairly static, predictable lives they may stay forever. If we're careless or move around a lot they don't, and we have to find new ones. We may need to go out actively looking and find only people who already have their friends in place and aren't in the market for more.

A bachelor acquaintance of mine said, "I don't have room for any more friends. Someone would have to die, to make a space."

A change of situation, like divorce or widowhood or a new job or a long-distance move, can open up a whole garden of new friends or else leave us totally isolated. The inspirational self-help books insist that it all depends on us, and if only we were a better kind of person we'd find the garden instead of the solitary cell, but they're dreaming. Much depends on the luck of the draw.

The right career helps. Some fields seem naturally friendlier; less suspicious, competitive, or isolating. Some work is so absorbing and exciting for its practitioners that almost any colleague will be a kinsman because of this shared passion. Many of the sciences and some of the arts fall into this category; edgy infighting may plague them, but the battles are companionable wars among equals, closed to outsiders. Corporate life tends to check in at the opposite end, and strugglers up the executive ladder aren't likely to find friends in the office; if they do, they'll need to be careful in conversation and stay mindful of politics.

For some solitaries, casual office contacts are most of the day's friendship ration. Lunches, complaints about the boss, interdepartmental gossip, updates on projects, the exchange of headache pills at the water cooler. This can be mildly sustaining, and occasionally grows into something personal. More often, though, either we or they move on to different jobs and the connection snaps; there's nothing left to talk about.

Extracurricular work and play can produce like-minded friends, or at least friendly acquaintances. Volunteering to teach the illiterate or clean up the roadsides. Learning bridge, or Arabic. Exercise is correct and popular now, and the virtuous spend time in gyms and health clubs, but this is by nature not a relaxing social atmosphere. People improving their muscles are so totally self-absorbed that they barely notice the other bodies in the room except to glance comparatively at their thighs.

America is short on friendly public places. The French have their cafés, the British their pubs, and sunny Latin countries turn out every evening to stroll and chat around a public square. We have the shopping mall, but it isn't quite the same, and making friends in malls seems reserved for teenagers. Bars in America feel slightly tainted by our ingrained Puritanism, slightly sinister—even, for solitary women, slightly disreputable. Not planned as amiable places to meet and chat with strangers, but places for businessmen to talk some quick business; for commuters reluctant to go home and grabbing a quick bracer; for the sexual adventurer to sign up someone for the night. For a brief time in the seventies it looked as if bars might evolve into something more leisurely, with wine and snacks, but then the sophisticated quit drinking anything but bottled water and started spending Happy Hour running in their shorts.

In cities, planned get-togethers, sponsored by everything from churches to dance studios, gather the solitaries in to socialize. Some are designed around a common interest, some specify only that members be single and have five dollars. Contrary to rumor, men do sometimes show up for these things; they tend to be nerds of purest ray serene. The women huddle together in bunches and complain about men, and ingratitude, and divorce lawyers.

In the city I sometimes think of as home, judging from the announcements in the newspaper, the only people having any fun are gays, lesbians, and ex-alcoholics, all of whom seem to meet and make friends gladly and go on interesting trips together. The rest of us are on our own.

Of course, not all friends are worth making. If we're desperate enough, and patient and cheerful and unselfish, we'll probably find a friend who wants to tell us things. This can be either male or female but more likely female, perhaps a married woman with secrets to confess and complaints about her husband, her family, her boredom, her parents. For some reason unattached people are considered suitable receptacles for these confidences. This friend has tales to tell, sometimes over and over, about the irritations and disappointments of her life; she has drinks and crackers for us, and winding paths of grievances to lead us down. She does not, however, want to hear about our troubles, and if we try to drag the conversation toward our own life her eyes glaze over and she remembers that the McIvers are coming for dinner and it's time for us to leave.

Then there's the opposite friend, who dearly loves to hear about our troubles, who thrives and grows plump and rosy on the worlds of other people. That's the advantage of friends; no real lady should have more than one husband or lover at a time, but we can cobble together a whole platform of different friends for different purposes.

The sympathetic friend appears as if by magic in time

of grief and disruption. She has advice, and the phone number of a really good therapist, and a man she wants us to meet. The man turns out to live with his mother and have trouble keeping a job, but the friend is a pearl beyond price. She calls up at exactly the crucial moment in the evening and says, "Are you all right? I just called to see if you're all right." She thinks hell isn't hot enough for our ex-lover. She calls and says, "You can come over if you like. Would you like to come over?" She listens to us until you'd think her ears would sag and drop off, and when she dies she will surely, surely be whisked directly into heaven through the main gate.

We begin to recover. We get a better job; we're seeing another, nicer man. The friend's gaze wanders, and one day she says, "Excuse me, I want to call Beverly. Poor Beverly, her husband's just gotten custody of the kid and she's completely destroyed. I want to call and make sure she's all right."

Different friends for different purposes.

There's the friend who's even needier than we are, and makes us feel brave and fortunate by comparison.

These lost souls are booby traps. They can be of either gender, and no matter what misfortune or carelessness has led them to their lonely rooms they never recover from it, never cheer up and take hold. Their days and nights are a frantic scramble to make someone else responsible for their lives. They can't entertain themselves for an hour. They can't even go out and buy a pair of shoes unless we're there to help decide. It's easy to catch an ankle in this trap: many of them are charming company at least some of the time, and it's cozy, for us without families, to feel so badly needed.

Then we go out of an evening without telling them, and come back to find the light on the answering machine flashing like the signal from a sinking ship. Were *are* we? We never *said* we were going out. Call as soon as we get in. The final message comes after we've gone to sleep and our needful friend has finished the vodka and is speaking fondly of suicide. Which is all our fault.

When we go to a party they're grieved that we didn't cadge an invitation for them too. Go away for a weekend without them and they're devastated. "Why didn't you *tell* me you and Debbie were going to the shore?" cried Muriel. "I'd have come with you."

I know.

I did go on a trip with Muriel, and it was fun. Once she had you firmly secured she was pleasant company. We came back and, as I was hauling my suitcase from the trunk of her car, she said we should make the same journey again at the same time next year. Every year, in fact.

She said she'd go straight home and make the reservations at once.

I fled.

Once these lost souls have their tentacles firmly around us, guilt helps hold us fast. Sometimes we can foist them off on someone else, or on a therapy group. If not, we'll learn our lesson: one thing worse than loneliness is being forced into someone's company against our will, and forced we are. We hold the thread that suspends them over the abyss; drop it at our peril.

Brutally, clumsily, I freed myself from Muriel. And she wasn't kidding. She did die. She died of drink, and loneliness, and rage against a world that had left her there alone. It happens. Not to us, though. Not to the brave.

Sometimes, with luck, we find the kind of true friend, male or female, that appears only two or three times in a lucky lifetime, one that will winter us and summer us, grieve, rejoice, and travel with us. These are the diamonds in our porridge.

Either friendships among women have come a long way in the last twenty years, or the way the world thinks of them and allows them has changed, or else we're just beginning to allow them ourselves. Until quite recently, they weren't acceptable to the men in our lives, and had to be kept quiet so as not to annoy them. Friendship between females over age fourteen was seen as hostile to men: what were we *talking* about together? Why, them, of course; what on earth else could there be to talk about? We must be exchanging secrets about them. Comparing their performances in bed. Betraying their private weaknesses. A woman without women friends was much desired, by men, and may still be, but perhaps we don't mind as much now. Perhaps what men think of us doesn't matter quite so acutely now.

Whatever the reasons, a group of women is no longer called a "hen party," as it once was, even by women. (Gatherings of men without women have always been called "stag parties." The difference between hens and stags says a mouthful.)

Traditionally, women sat and talked with their friends, perhaps because for many it was hard to get away from that kitchen table; somebody might need something. In generations past, ashamed of idleness, they might all be shelling peas, snapping beans, darning socks, or peeling apples, mindless occupations that lend themselves to chat of personal matters. Men went out and did things with their friends—played golf, poker, softball; caught fish; shot deer; hunted mastodons—and their conversation, if any, was confined to the project at hand. This distinction may be changing, though it's hard to tell. Single women do seem to be starting to collect skiing buddies, tennis buddies, biking buddies, even aerobics buddies. Perhaps somewhere single men are sitting at a kitchen table together exchanging intimate complaints and gossip; stranger things have happened. It's all to the good. Friendships, for the single, need all the dimensions they can get.

They need working on, too. Friends differ from families in that friends require maintenance. Families, like it or not, are always there, which is the point of families. If you want to see them you don't need to call up and make arrangements to see them. They rarely leave town without letting you know. When they're around, you don't need to entertain them; if you have something to say, you say it, otherwise not. If you quarrel with family you can sulk for days, because sooner or later, over the matter of a dentist appointment or a television program or who needs the car, you find yourself speaking again and the quarrel fades and vanishes. A quarrel with resident family is a great nuisance to keep up, but the briefest tiff with a friend can last forever; you can't call up three days later and say, "Looks as if we might have some rain." Mending it takes a conscious, deliberate, even embarrassing act. You have to take steps to patch it up.

My friend Annabel lost a lifelong friend over the matter of being late showing up in front of a movie theater. A few crisp words were exchanged, and then somehow the days went by, and turned into months, and now it's been several years. Very likely they will never see each other again.

Fracturing or even loosening the bonds of family takes considerable effort, but the filaments of friendship are delicate. Ignore them for a few months and they shrivel and blow away. You have to call up and say, "Hi, I just called to say hello." Nothing continues of its own momentum.

For some, friendship begins to seem like too much work. As connections break one by one, they lose the will to tie new ones, and loneliness scabs over like an old wound and hardens into isolation: the door on the chain, the eye at the crack; whatever it is, I'm not interested. Go away.

For the solitary, friendship is how we fasten ourselves to the human community; if we let it go we end up dangling in space, but if we tend and strengthen and widen it, we're in stronger contact than our sisters locked away in stable families. It can lead us into worlds we never knew, and put our hands on different textures, and keep opening up new angles on the view. It can make us active members of the world the way our jobs have done. Owing no private, primary allegiance, we're at liberty to sign up our affections where we please and follow them as far as we like. We can make friends that would horrify any proper spouse. It makes us strong. We learn things, and learning keeps us awake.

Friendship favors the extroverted and the self-confident, and it favors women. Women have it better than men. Much is made of what's currently called male bonding, but this tends to be wordless, sometimes curiously impersonal, and often, as noted, based on doing something together, oftener in groups than in pairs, and often something competitive, with winners and losers. Whether it's nature or nurture, it seems to be true that a deep streak of competition hampers men's friendships. They need to save face, to deny defeat. A man in emotional trouble is more likely to cry for help from a woman than from another man, and his male friends are less likely to call up and ask him if he's okay or would he like to come over and talk; it might be considered an insult.

A man's circle of friends may be so impersonal that replacing one is as easy as finding a new first baseman for the softball club. Emotional depth is suspect, possibly from a fear of homosexuality. A recent study showed that only one third of all single men queried would admit to having a "best friend," and among these most of the best friends were women.

As time passes, men find it harder to make new friends, too, and can keep coasting dully through the years with the same college and business contacts they've always had. Not necessarily loved and treasured old chums, either; just familiar, saying the same old things, easier to keep than replace.

Women, on the other hand, keep up a lively interest in new people and go on making friends through life. For obvious reasons, mothers find a whole rush of new friendships as soon as they get the children out of their hair. By the time they're old enough to be called "old," women with one good friend are stronger and happier, according to research, than women surrounded by grandchildren but good-friendless.

All very well, but on rainy evenings this may still seem like cold comfort. The strongest among us may still whine for love, true love, and the prince who is mommy and daddy and husband and brother and will never leave our sides. Those who have had and lost princes or families may slide tearfully into nostalgia, and sit for hours summoning up the songs of long ago, snapshot visions of small children playing on a beach, the scratch of a morning beard or sun on a breakfast table, as if sheer concentration might reassemble the past and give it flesh.

And probably there's no Santa Claus either. Go out and pick up a movie with Cary Grant in it, come back and put the kettle on. Tomorrow we'll get by. With, of course, a little help from our friends.

Chapter 4

Children

James James
Morrison Morrison
Weatherby George Dupree
Took great
Care of his Mother,
Though he was only three.

—A. A. MILNE

Sometimes parents without resident partners complain that they, too, live alone, but they don't. Solitude doesn't mean the absence of a live-in companion of the opposite sex; solitude is when you're all by yourself.

Certainly raising children single-handed has its problems, but they aren't the same problems. Female parents alone worry about money. Nearly half of them fall below the poverty line. They have less time to sit around brooding about their loneliness because they're brooding about how to keep Rice Krispies on the table and sneakers on the feet. Of the eight single mothers I've known well, raising a total of twenty children among them, only one has cashed regular, dependable support checks from an ex-husband. These aren't statistics, of course, just friends, and I may have friends with peculiarly bad taste in husbands, but still it seems odd among such a respectable, middle-class group. Statistically, a woman's standard of living plunges by about seventy percent after divorce, while her husband's jumps by thirty or forty percent. Add children, and we're talking serious penny-pinching.

Back in an agricultural world, even quite young children could earn their keep with chores; more recently, young teenagers worked after school and on weekends delivering newspapers or groceries or pumping gas, and some contributed to the family income. This custom seems to have died out. Teenagers now work in fast-food eateries and spend the proceeds on clothes, though not the kind of clothes they take for granted, like sneakers and warm jackets. Financially speaking, children are a liability.

None of my single-mother friends falls into the job categories we read about in upscale magazines; none of them brings home legal briefs to study on the weekend, or comes home late after high-powered executive meetings. They're hunters and gatherers, scrambling for what they can pick up and trying to avoid day care and sitters by beating the school bus home. Sometimes they're driving the school bus. They deliver mail, clean houses, drop off copies of the Yellow Pages, take census data, badger people by phone to sign up for credit cards, tutor math, teach calligraphy, and wait on tables in cocktail lounges wearing indecent costumes. So far, knock wood, only one has failed and lost everything.

Sally really wasn't making it. She was very young and bewildered and had three very young children, and someone told her to take a computer course. She scrounged and scurried around and managed, somehow, with kindly neighbors watching her kids. She completed the course. Then she couldn't find a job. Presently her stinker of an ex-husband swooped down and put the house up for sale, gathered up the kids, and went away. Sally, having nothing left but her clothes, went off to a faraway state to live with her parents. She should have sued her lawyer, or had his kneecaps broken, but as I said she was young, and never did have a firm grip on the ways of the world.

Up until recently, if a woman had custody of the children, their father had something called "visitation rights," which are apparently better than mere visiting rights, though only a lawyer could tell you why; I always thought visitations glowed with an eerie light and told you to make a pilgrimage and then vanished. Legal visitation meant that Father came over on at least some Saturday afternoons and asked the children what they'd been doing in school; the children said "Nothing," and squirmed, and the father and mother pretended to smile at each other.

Under newer arrangements, the children are shared. Sometimes the father has them on weekends, which complicates his social life but gives the mother a nice break. Sometimes the parents live near each other, and the children spend a week here and a week there, lugging their teddy bears from house to house. This has various results, since parents have various notions on child raising. If they live in the same house they can fight it out day by day; if they live separately, the kids have to learn to change gears en route.

The parents do some gear changing too. A week surrounded by clutter and clamor, followed by a week of silence, sometimes quivering with jealousy, curiosity, and general angst. The part-time parent never quite comes to grips with the devices and solaces of solitude. She or he doesn't have time. It does, though, offer some time to work on one's love life.

For the full-time mother alone with small children, the search for a romantic partner gets lost in a scuffle of homework and Pampers and laundry. One said to me recently, briskly, "I don't have time to fall in love. What I really need is a man to stop by once a week, at bedtime. Or a man I could just call when I need him, like an electrician." Most therapists would tell her this is a selfish and emotionally unsound attitude, and she ought to make time to go looking for a meaningful adult relationship. (Therapists tend to discount the meaningfulness of relations with children, as well as the short leashes of seekers with a two-year-old at home.)

Children complicate the mechanics of sex, lovers, and finding new husbands and wives to replace the lost ones. Some prospective lovers are embarrassed by children, and some are downright repelled. It helps if one's kids are reasonably calm and clean, and trained to answer when spoken to and not to climb on your guests or put turtles down their backs. (On the other hand, if you find a lover who can take a turtle in the shirt with equanimity, you've found something special. Kids give you a broader chance to assess the prospect.)

Then there are baby-sitters. They make dating expensive.

Then there's guilt. Guilt at going out on dates and leaving the children, who see so little of you anyway. Guilt at staying home on dates, an obvious lover in front of their curious eyes. I know a single father whose new love waited six months to get her foot across his threshold, and another three before he'd let her stay the night.

Guilt darkens the situation. A parent who lies and apologizes finds the kids agreeing; why blush and bluster like that if it isn't a dreadful thing to do? In the households that look the sturdiest and most successful, the parent takes a cheerful, matter-of-fact stance on sex, and lovers hang around and help paint the living room; go out for the Sunday papers; fry bacon.

One woman I know broke up with her lover after a year or so, and her son now goes to spend weekends with him. They go fishing together.

Another, raising four teenage sons in a disheveled, crumbling old house in the country, grieves over the need to change lovers as new work needs doing on the house. She said a sad farewell to the one who'd fixed the roof, because the back-bedroom ceiling fell down and she had to take up with a plastering fellow instead, the budget having no slack in it for plasterers. Her sons urged her to have both, being fond of the roofer, but she felt this was unladylike. Now the front porch has started to sag, and she's looking around again.

Some of us, with our babes at our knees, have trouble finding lovers anywhere; we meet only men impatient of the smallest inconvenience, and unlikely to put up with the shriek of a nightmare in the other bedroom while they're making love.

Ideally, single mothers should be able to find single

fathers, and merge, but the odds are against it. There simply aren't enough single fathers to go around, and if you did find one, your two sets of offspring would probably take an instant, violent loathing to each other. Even if they didn't, the two of you, each used to being the only authority, have probably developed a lot of ironclad and radically different whims on things like pillow fights and table manners. Fur would fly.

In spite of all the drawbacks, though, it seems that my childed friends find nicer lovers than the rest of us, and keep them longer. There's a group of men out there who could use a bit of mothering themselves, and instead of feeling that the kids are soaking it all up, they feel free to share in it. They see you packing lunchboxes and combing hair, and they feel cozy. Unthreatened by the leftover hostilities of the great liberation. Less bristly than they feel with crisply dressed lady executives. Free to ask for comfort, and maybe even give you a hand with the dishes without losing face.

I don't know what separates these pleasant souls from the child-resenters. Maybe something to do with their birth order. Anyway, if you find one, you may wind up feeling you've simply acquired an extra child, but there's nothing wrong with that either.

The full-time single father with younger children is in

the soup, no matter how amiably sentimental we may feel about him. Nannies are only for millionaires. My friend Paul isn't a millionaire, but he does have a high-powered job that calls for long-distance traveling and, during his sojourns at home, dinner meetings and executive tennis. This sounds like the plushy life, and surely all he had to do was hire someone, and he did. Someone, after someone, after someone. Live in, live out, stop by. They came and they went, usually without warning. They failed to show up for any of a thousand creative reasons. They stole everything they could carry. Paul's life tangled itself into a nightmare of marathon sitters who were supposed to take over from each other at stated intervals. A man at a sales meeting in Baltimore who gets a phone call from an eight-year-old in San Diego sobbing that Maria never showed up to make dinner is not a happy man.

It never crossed his mind to get a different sort of job. That job was his achievement, his life, and leaving it would have been psychic suicide.

This isn't usually a single mother's dilemma. Statistically she's pretty unlikely to be offered a job like Paul's to begin with—women make up less than 1 percent of the country's top management—and if it were offered, she'd be likely to turn it down. Occasionally we read about a man who's throttling back his career to spend more time with his children, but I wouldn't call it an epidemic just yet. For all the changes in the air, motherhood still feels like a primary job for a woman and fatherhood like a secondary job for a man. Men expect to have something to show for their work, like money; the rewards of parenting are nebulous.

Some problems get easier as the kids grow. Sometimes an adolescent, angry at its mother or depressed by her restricted life and budget, may elect to go live with its father, and this can turn out well for all parties. One of the most successful single-parent households I know is a man with a boy and girl in their mid-teens. He doesn't fuss over psychological problems best left unplumbed, or wonder whether they're happy or even whether they like him. He runs a tight ship, and concerns himself with report cards, tidiness, promptness, and obedience. To a woman, there's an air of the military school about it; a straitjacket of tasks and timetables and complicated punishments for infractions of minor rules, but the kids seem to be flourishing. He doesn't confide in them or tell them his troubles. There's no question of his being a friend; he's a father. In return, he leaves them air space to grow in. To younger children, though, this same air space might feel cold and drafty.

Single fathers apparently don't consider their children

company; single mothers do. A man who's been married feels that a house without a woman is scarcely a house at all, and even knee-deep in a waste of hockey sticks and doll clothes he considers himself alone. Have lunch with him, and after he's answered your polite queries about his young, he goes on to talk about a woman he's seeing, or problems at the office. Have lunch with a single mother and the conversation's likely to begin and end with Valerie's first-grade teacher and Ian's sinuses. Single mothers, scrabbling for money and dashing out of the office to a teachers' conference, can forget to keep up their own friendships and settle down to be visibly content with their laps full of young, their heads full of orthodontia and spelling bees, at least for the time being. A mother can make herself a nest out of kids.

Sometimes a woman who, for one reason or another, has given up expecting the prince, may wonder why she can't have children either. Is childlessness a punishment for having failed to secure a man? Having snatched one promised sweet away, the fates reach out and snatch the other with the other hand. It's catch-23: having no husband, we're in particular need of children, for company and the human connection, but having no husband we can't have the children that, if we had a husband, we wouldn't need as much.

Thirty or forty years ago, having a child on one's own was actually a more practical option than it is now. An energetic woman with a steady job could manage by herself, and the social repercussions weren't as dire as you might think. To have a lover and accidentally find yourself pregnant out of wedlock was very wrong, but to find the biologically necessary father and have a child because you wanted a child was much more acceptable. Accidental pregnancy meant a girl had been overcome by disgraceful, unfeminine lust; deliberate pregnancy meant she wanted the one thing all proper women were supposed to want.

My ex-husband grew up in the 1940s in a socially conservative, God-fearing midwestern town where the county librarian, a maiden lady of blameless life, found someone—she never gave out his name—to father a child for her. No one threatened her job, or crossed to the other side of the street, and the child grew up without stigma. My ex-husband remembers the town's silent pride in such a determined, well-organized, unabashed woman who'd beaten the odds and managed to have at least half a life instead of no life at all, by the standards of the time.

Today, except in a few fringe circles where everything goes, it's harder socially. Forty years ago it was accepted that, because mothers raised children, having a child was a woman's own business. Now fathers are considered at least half the equation, and a woman who brings a child into the world without a resident male parent is a selfish beast, depriving it in advance of half its parenting. The very suggestion of deliberate single motherhood, in a recent syndicated advice column, brought a firestorm of outraged mail. The climate may change, but currently the country is deeply attached to something called family values. Politicians praise them highly, though no one has explained what they are, exactly. What they aren't, obviously, is having a fatherless child on purpose.

However, no one has suggested that you can't marry the next toad on your doorstep, conceive, and divorce. This makes the whole enterprise more complicated but respectable: after all, you tried.

The real hurdle nowadays is money. It's cheaper to have a yacht than a child. Look at all the harried married mothers, stopping by the day-care center on the way to the office; today's children need food, clothing, shelter, and a two-income family. The price went up. *American Demographics* pegged the 1989 cost of baby's first year at $5,774. Back in 1958, *Life* magazine figured it at $800. Adjust that for inflation to 1989 and you'd have just $2,892, or nearly $3,000 less than the actual price tag.

By the age of eighteen, baby will have set you back

over $135,000, according to the Department of Agriculture. Then there's college.

And that's just *one* child.

Those single women who still want one but find pregnancy too complicated can look at the adoption option. You don't get first pick, of course. Sane, healthy, normal, eligible infants can afford to be choosy, and the parents of choice are sane, healthy, normal, young, stable married couples, and even they often wait for years. Single, you aren't even in the running. You can apply for children with what they call "special needs," which are heartbreakingly various and could be so pressing that you'd have trouble holding down a job while you dealt with them. Or you can look abroad. According to the National Committee for Adoption, in Washington, D.C., foreign adoptions more than doubled in the 1980s, and they're often faster and easier than local arrangements. There's no guarantee that your foreign child will be perfect, any more than there is with your own child, and it may have special needs too. It too may have tantrums and destroy the house, and do it in Spanish, or in some dialect that no one in your school system understands any better than you do.

Wherever your child or children came from, schools will become a powerful influence in your life. The price estimates of raising children don't include private secondary school, which may easily cost twice as much as you paid for college. If the public system where you live is terrifying, and fewer than half the students graduate or even live that long, you'll need to move. A child with a literate, strong, interested mother can probably manage in a bad elementary school, but by middle-school level you'll have to get out. This usually means moving to the suburbs, which can be as cold and lonely as the moon to single women, and involves commuting, a reliable car, sitters, and often a hefty mortgage.

Some city school systems have pilot or magnet schools or schools with entrance examinations, to try to keep the middle class in town, but don't rely on these too heavily. One of the brightest kids I know came down with flu on the day of the entrance exam, and staggered conscientiously off with a high fever to take it anyway. He did badly. If he'd stayed in bed, he'd have been eligible for the makeup exam, but having taken the first exam, he wasn't. He didn't get in.

That's the trouble with children. Anything can happen and usually does.

The other thing to remember is that children are temporary. As soon as they develop a sense of humor and get to be good company, maybe even remember to take the trash out and close the refrigerator door, they pack up their electronic equipment and their clothes, and some of your clothes, and leave in a U-Haul, to return only at

Thanksgiving. They were just passing through; they were always just passing through, on their way to their own lives.

If you get a healthy kitten and take good care of it, it will last you as long as the average child and cost less.

Sometimes, nowadays, children come back after they've left. After you've rearranged your life and adjusted to their absence, maybe learned to love it, they rush back into the empty nest with all their belongings tied up in a sheet, pursued by misalliance or misfortune or high rents. Married couples complain bitterly about this, but single parents usually readjust. It's a blast of different air and different music, another generation storming in and out. Of course it can be flattening when they all dash off to a movie or a weekend outing without asking if you'd like to come. Well, naturally you wouldn't, you'd feel like a fool, maybe, surrounded by the young and their friends, but not being asked makes you feel subhuman, a non-person unimaginably remote from normal pursuits.

Still, they keep your slang up to date and open a different window.

After you've readjusted, they leave again.

Sometimes they come back with children of their own, but that puts you a long way beyond the scope of this discussion.

At any of their various stages, having children around

complicates life, but the oversimplified life can be pretty deadly. Children vary the days, rough up the flatness, and keep you from getting too comfortable.

They fasten you to the world. When you write a school absence excuse, or make a Halloween costume, or shop for their jeans, you're part of the larger scheme of things, connected to the moving parts of the social machine. A man feels that way about his job, no matter what it is; the sales rep in gents' underwear believes with all his heart that his work is an essential element in the world's functioning, but for women only certain jobs qualify as important. Most women know in their hearts that if they keeled over at their desks, they'd be replaced by Monday, and the world would go ticking along without them, or even if they weren't replaced it wouldn't matter very much. A child needs its mother and can't replace her through a classified ad.

With less dignity to protect than a man, a woman can sit on the floor and play Monopoly or Lotto, and even, with an older child, talk over a few problems. The roller skate on the stairs, the homework on the kitchen table, keep her chin up. She can't be scared, or at least can't admit it. She can't quit trying, give up, or skip dinner— or town. If she cries, she has to do it quietly, in bed.

Cats and dogs and parakeets are all very well, but they don't connect us to anything beyond our own walls.

We're responsible for the pet itself, but that's a private contract; with a kid, we're responsible to the world.

Children have their points. If you haven't any, you might consider getting one. After you win the lottery, maybe.

Chapter 5

Shelter

And hie him home, at evening's close,
To sweet repast and calm repose.

—THOMAS GRAY

Most people alone live in apartments in cities, because it's convenient and there are things to do and faces to look at and other people around us living alone so we needn't feel peculiar. If we're newly out of college or newly divorced or widowed, acquiring this apartment may be our first contact, or our first in years, with rental agents.

No one knows why rental agents are the way they are. They may have been abused as children, or it may be inborn, a wild gene zigzagging through the generations. As far as anyone knows, it's incurable. Rental agents are unable to write you the simplest letter about something ordinary, like a change in the water rates, without adding that your failure to instantly comply will result in you and yours being cast out into the winter streets; your furniture will be sold at auction, and if in the process he catches you with a cat, or even an ant farm, the cat will be strangled and the ants flushed down the toilet.

Some people can't even read their leases without crying.

Minimize contact. Don't ask rental agents annoying questions—and most questions annoy them. If you point out that the air conditioner in your prospective home is broken, he will ask you if you think he looks like an air-conditioner repairman. If you wonder aloud why the refrigerator door is half off its hinges, he will retort that refrigerators in apartments are a gift, a present offered only through his personal kindness and generosity, and if you don't like it you're free to buy your own.

Most rental agents are too busy writing nasty letters to their current tenants to be bothered walking prospective tenants around town looking at apartments, and it's just as well. They let you take the keys, often in exchange for something valuable like your driver's license or your arm, and go look for yourself.

Nothing about an empty apartment in the modest price range encourages a bright view of one's future. Looking at three or four in a single day can bring on acute melancholia. Sometimes it helps to take along a friend for moral support; sometimes it just reduces you both to despair.

The cost of convenient city shelter, like the cost of raising children, has gone up. Apartments once considered suitable for students, young people in their first jobs, and women living alone have been polished up to sell as condos to two-income childless couples. Violent crime in the streets has skyrocketed along with the rents. Once upon a time a cheap apartment was merely dark and cramped, far from offices and shopping, and three flights up. Now it's all those things and dangerous too. A woman alone will need to spend more than she wants to just to live in a place she can leave after dark. Spend the extra even if you have to eat boiled beans forever; nothing is worse for us than life in the isolation of fear and helplessness.

In choosing an apartment, beware of panic. Something about simply *needing* a place to live unhinges judgment and recycles our childhood nightmares. We're Hansel and Gretel cast out in the woods. Snow White running from her wicked stepmother, brambles snatching at our clothes. The Little Match Girl freezing in the streets. We're Adam and Eve thrown out of the Garden; we're the Wandering Jew; we're a stray cat looking for a cranny out of the wind, and we're apt to settle for the first cranny we can find.

If we're looking because of some upheaval in our life, the sense of homelessness and frantic urgency can lead us into some odd and awful places. If we're simply sick of the place we have, we're usually more deliberate. Look at more places; case different neighborhoods on foot; weigh the trade-offs. Choose thoughtfully between the one with the primitive kitchen and splendid view and the one with the eat-in kitchen that faces a filthy concrete wall. Bear in mind that once we're there, it won't go *on* looking like that, with the torn window blind and the empty paint cans and the celery fermenting in the vegetable crisper. We'll bring our own things. Hang curtains. Give a party. Find a dry cleaner and a drugstore. Make it feel like home.

Every year, 20 percent of all Americans move out from under one roof and in under another. For us who live alone the percentage is higher. We're a restless lot, and we don't stay put because the children are used to it here; we move on because things might be better somewhere else. "I've never cleaned an oven," said a friend of mine. "When the oven needs cleaning it's time to move."

We learn to pay attention to the metaphors, the irrational factors that stand for our private myths. These can lean hard on our lives without ever quite announcing themselves aloud. Morning sun, for instance, means hope and rebirth, energy and bright promise and a happy day to come. Afternoon sun, when we reach a certain age, means decline. My friend Heidi, at forty, turned down a perfectly splendid apartment because of its westward windows through which that evenin' sun went down. All-day darkness from the north or tall buildings means loneliness and sorrow. For the strong, an apartment on a high floor, with a view of the backs of flying birds, means achievement, the conquering of heights; for the frail and hesitant it means falling through empty space. Basements mean failure, as in the baseball team in the basement that hasn't won a game since June. They also mean burial, and a place where vermin go to hide.

Challenging flights of stairs are good exercise but isolating. The metaphor here is Fair Rosamund and the Lady of Shalott and Rapunzel, all locked away from the world in their towers, and it's more than just metaphor. People think twice about dropping in on you—if "dropping" isn't the wrong word—and you think twice before stepping out for a stroll or a visit. Once you're there, you're there.

A fourth-floor bachelor I know has made quite a reputation for his home-brewed beer; he says it's easier to make his own than to go out for a six-pack and climb back home again.

Out at the far ends of the commuting lines you can find respectable apartments at more reasonable rates, but these wear an eerie sense of being nowhere at all. The apartments themselves were built for cost-efficiency; cream-colored boxes, people-containers; the inhabitants are part of no town, no city. The place around them exists only so that they can travel to it, lie down and sleep, then rise again and leave it for the real world. The space may be a great bargain, but it's no home for the single.

In most older cities you can choose between apartment buildings and the remodeled houses built originally for families with half a dozen children, servants, and a maiden aunt. The big building means the safety of invisible masses of neighbors and a watchdog doorman to keep the riffraff out. It can also mean sterility and facelessness; all those neighbors have no names. The brownstone, in addition to high ceilings, solid doors, and decorative cornices, holds out the promise of friendship and sociability. Also the promise of bitter wrenching feuds with crazed neighbors who lie in wait in the halls to harangue us.

Haunted by the unknowable factors, we have to make

a choice. We consider two apartments, and our future unrolls into mystery from each. Next door to the first apartment lives the love of our life, waiting behind his door for the chance meeting in the hall, when he holds our groceries for us while we rummage for our key. Next door to the second lives the wicked witch, cackling and brewing curses. Which is which? We spring blindfolded into our future; sign the lease.

The rental agent gives us a wintry smile and reminds us of the 10 percent fine if the check isn't in his hands on the first of the month.

Now we can go away and read the fine print. As the leases in one's life mount up, they begin to seem less threatening. I've never known anyone who was actually evicted for any of the listed reasons except not paying the rent. Most of those hostile clauses are simply there because they're there, have always been on leases since time and rents began; they're traditional. My last lease threatened me with eviction if I stored ashes on the property, a nostalgic reminder of coal furnaces or maybe wood-burning stoves.

Leases can even be broken. If you're brave, you can go in person to the rental agent and tell him your aunt in Denver is paralyzed and you have to go live with her. However, even if he believes you, he'll expect rent for every hour it takes him to find a new tenant, and if you've been living in a place a stray dog wouldn't live in, it won't be soon. You can also leave quietly, by night, with some strong friends helping; what's known as a midnight flit. I've done it several times and lived to tell the tale. Presumably the rental agent puts your name out on the streets as an undesirable tenant, and other agents either worry about this or they don't, depending on how badly they need you.

Then there's the matter of pets. No one knows why, in America, alone of all nations, landlords hate animals. All animals. The bulletin board at the vet's office is deeply crusted with sad messages from people trying to unload their pets because the new lease forbids them. Docilely, timorously, people send their dear old fur-bearing friends to the gas chamber because of a rental agent or a landlord. In Europe, in Russia, all over the civilized world, it's taken for granted that people need what the psychologists call a companion animal. The medical establishment agrees unanimously that those who live alone absolutely require one, for reasons of sanity. Pet-facilitated therapy, or PFT, has moved into nursing and convalescent homes. Studies show that people who touch and talk to their pets have fewer problems with high blood pressure, and recover more quickly and survive longer after heart attacks.

We need them. Overwhelmingly, in rented apartments, even rented houses, even condos, we can't have them.

It seems so arbitrary that I tried to argue with a rental agent once, a foolish thing to do.

"Pets make messes," he explained, gazing proudly down at an expanse of khaki-colored plastic carpeting, the kind that gives you rope burns if you go barefoot. "It's new," he said. "We just had it installed. Cats would make messes on it."

"No, they wouldn't," I said with spirit, having already decided against the dreary place.

"Oh, it's not the cats' fault," he said. "It's the owners'. They don't discipline them properly."

"You don't know much about cats," I retorted. "And besides, what if they did make messes? You don't have any rules against kids—suppose I moved in with a four-year-old and he walked jelly into the carpet? Suppose I spilled spaghetti sauce on it? You'd have it cleaned, or get a new one, and take it out of the security deposit. Can't cat damage come out of a security deposit? And if pets were a nuisance, a cat yowled or a dog barked, isn't that the same as noisy parties? You'd just say shut up or get out, wouldn't you?"

He turned away, bored; a crazy lady. "It's a rule we have in all our buildings," he said. "No pets. Period."

Once I signed a kindlier lease that said I could

have cats to the number of two, or a single dog weigh-
ing less than twenty pounds, for a surcharge of twenty-
five dollars a month apiece. At no extra charge, I could
have another *person* living with me, giving noisy parties
and spilling spaghetti sauce, but my cat had to pay
three hundred nonrefundable dollars a year just in case
she had an accident on those battered, uncarpeted
floors. On top, of course, of the security deposit in
case *I* had an accident on them. And I suppose the dog
of under twenty pounds would have to check in for
regular reweighing, in case he overate and exceeded the
limit.

I asked the rental agent about this curious rule, and
he explained that once, in another building, years ago, a
tenant had had a dog that shed fur in the halls. The minds
of rental agents move in mysterious ways.

Later I rented a townhouse with a lease that said not
even a goldfish could join me there, not even a transient
goldfish. What with one thing and another, I accumulated five cats, many of whom crowded onto the first-
floor windowsill to make their presence known. I lived
guiltily under the shadow of eviction, paying my rent
promptly and taking care of repairs myself, to forestall
discovery.

Hundreds of thousands of more law-abiding solitaries
obey their leases, and come home from work to an

empty apartment with no companion to greet them at the door.

I'm in favor of defiance, myself. After all, if enough of us simply ignored the clause, as everyone would in France or England, how many of us could they evict, and for how long could they hold out against us, brooding self-righteously in their empty buildings?

If civil disobedience doesn't appeal to you, you can leave town. There are options out there beyond the beltways, in the suburbs, and even in the country. You can go look at houses; you can think about buying.

Violent crime is rarer out there. You can leave the house in safety after dark, though you may find fewer reasons for doing so. You can have all the pets you want, except, in the suburbs, pigs or lions. You can plant flowers. You too can be that ultimate grownup, the home-owner, even if the prince or princess has been late arriving.

There will be space, blessed space. No longer will you keep knocking over the trash and stepping in the cat's dish whenever you reach for something in the kitchen. People can give you birthday presents—African violets, large fantasy dragons in papier-mâché, a food processor—and there'll be somewhere to put them besides the floor.

You can call your soul your own. Bid farewell to the rental agent, that father figure from hell, and paint the walls in purple stripes if you want. You can fix the place up. After the first few rented places, the urge to refurbish and build shelves begins to fade: you aren't making yourself a home, you're just doing the undeserving management a favor. A home of one's own can be a soul-satisfying hobby.

It's tempting. Miriam, a free-lance graphics designer I know, was tempted and fell. After a series of long, anxious-making, inconclusive love affairs she decided to take her life in her own hands and buy herself a house.

Houses are expensive, of course. When she finally found one she could afford, it was on the outskirts of town, neither here nor there, neither in the cheering bustle of city life nor the all-American dreaming green of the suburbs. Still it was a house, with a real garage for her car and a bit of a lawn, and she loved it. Getting the mortgage was the sweetest compliment she'd had in years, and surprising, too, since free-lancing women aren't the darlings of mortgage-givers. She felt full-grown at last.

It didn't work out. The neighborhood was no slum, but it was tough working-class, suspicious and insular. Miriam was an unmarried woman in her thirties, unheard of in that part of town, and a bubbly blonde who claimed to earn her living drawing pictures. The block felt something fishy was definitely going on. Coarse remarks were overheard. Children threw trash on her lawn, and twice she set out rows of petunias, to find them gray and gasping on the sidewalk next morning. Miriam lost her temper and shouted at some loitering kids, and after that the situation deteriorated, as they say in the State Department. She grew paranoid. The hostility around her penetrated the walls and darkened her neat cozy living room. Finally, after what happened on Halloween, she moved back to an apartment and put the house on the market.

The problem isn't always so ugly; it can be merely deadening. Another and better-paid woman I know, with a doctorate in a respectable science, took an excellent job in a midwestern city and bought a nicer house than Miriam's, in a nicer neighborhood. She was simply ignored. Walking her dog mornings and evenings, she felt invisible. Local activities, such as they were, revolved around the schools and various churches she didn't belong to. There was nothing she could join and no way to meet people, perhaps no people who wanted to meet her, and after a couple of years of invisibility she quit the job and moved back where she'd come from.

As a general rule, the more sophisticated the area, the

more acceptable it is to be living alone, and the more likely we are to be among friends.

Not that a city building full of other solitaries is any guarantee. Again, it's the luck of the draw. I once spent two years in a brownstone of one-room apartments, where each room seemed to contain its own hell of peculiarity, except perhaps mine; my life at the time was hectic but sane and enlivened by lovers. I shared the third floor with a man whose name, according to the mailbox, was Moody. He had no visitors, and never said hello as he scurried through the halls with an air of furtive busyness. His hobby was newspapers. Glimpsed through the opening door, his apartment's only furniture, other than the wallowing mountains of old newspapers, was a bright red Coca-Cola chest from the days before vending machines. It was big enough to contain at least one corpse, and its lid was held down by several thousand browning newspapers. I could see a bit of the bathroom; the tub was four feet deep in ancient newsprint.

Below me lived a melancholy bachelor who presently gave up on independence and moved back home with his mother, to be replaced by Kay, who often called the police to complain that the rest of us were vibrating the building to keep her from sleeping. Then there was the man in 2B who turned on the gas and had to be snatched from the doorstep of death; I've forgotten his name.

Perhaps the building was infested with evil spirits. Perhaps a psychic advisor could have warned me off. These matters are mysterious: my next apartment was in a building that looked, from the outside, almost exactly the same except for its street number, but it was filled with merry and pleasant souls who stopped to chat and left their doors ajar for my cat to come and visit.

A single woman with children may need to live in the suburbs, for the schools, and for her the children make contact and help her seem less peculiar, more identifiable. They give her something to talk about with the married world, and school plays and PTA meetings to go to. She's unlikely to find a marvelous man to marry, but she may easily find married men with whom to have affairs. These are amazingly difficult to keep secret in the suburbs, and when they're discovered the social repercussions are quite disagreeable and the children will suffer from them.

A single man in the suburbs will find married women to have affairs with, and he's more likely to get invited to dinner. Even curmudgeonly bachelors have a certain glamour, for both sexes, in a heavily married area, and a single father with children at home will have neighbors taking a kindly, officious interest in his parenting. Given the talents and the energy, he can work up quite a pleasant social life for himself, and throw sophisticated little parties. He makes a nice change. Somehow, unmarried women just don't.

No one is quite clear what makes the difference between a suburb and a small town; many suburbs were once small towns before the city swarmed over them. Basically, a town is farther from a city and commuting is inconvenient enough to give the place some independent life, with available jobs and a volunteer fire department. A town contains more people who have lived there all their lives, went to school there, and married schoolmates. Because it isn't dangling from the umbilical cord of a city, it has a consoling sense of place. Towns can be soothing. If you know people who already live in one, people with an accepted position there, who can vouch for your character and get you into the Shakespeare Club or the Sewing Circle and introduce you to the Rotary Club, it's something to think about.

Out beyond where the sidewalks stop there's the country, the real country, with owls in the trees and field mice in the attic. There are times, maybe after we've had our wallet lifted or our car window smashed, or the cockroaches have come bustling back with their friends and relations, or a derelict has moved into the vestibule and the rent's gone up again, when visions of country life can glow like El Dorado. Not for everyone, of course; an urban friend of mine says firmly, "The country is the place where little animals come and die on your doorstep, and you find them there in the morning." I have found much worse things on my city doorstep, but it's true that for some the country is a metaphor for exile.

For others, it's a place to get back to the Four First Things: earth, air, fire, and water. You can raise vegetables and even animals for food, giving yourself a false but comforting sense of independence. My friend Diane lives in the country, with a vegetable garden and a barn, and at night, before she goes to bed, she takes the dogs out for a final run and stands there on her lane and looks up at the stars. There are chickens in the barn, and a pair of geese and a goat, and it's true they aren't human but they're hers. In the city, you can see all those people streaming by, and it's true they're human but they aren't yours.

Socially, you won't be considered as odd in the country as in the suburbs, partly because there are fewer neighbors to consider you at all and partly because the countryside wasn't built on purpose to house the nuclear family the way the suburbs were. There were always solitaries out there. We all have a vision of the crusty widower on his porch with a shotgun across his knees in case of visitors; the toothless crone with her bedroom full of hens.

You won't be shunned in the country, but you may find it slow going to make new friends. Your neighbors may be suspicious of all newcomers, and afraid of the social contaminants—liberalism, homosexuality, AIDS, martinis—that may follow in your wake. The warmth and helpfulness of country folk is partly legend, left over from the pre-car, pre-telephone days when neighbors needed each other more than they do today. In the worst-case scenario, you may find a lot of men whose most intense relationships are with their trucks and their guns, and women whose deepest feelings are for their washing machines and the characters in television dramas.

In the summer, your city friends can come visit you, and in the winter you can pay them back. Winters are several months longer out there, to be replaced finally, gradually, by mud season.

Still, solitaries have moved to the country and flourished there, and grown accustomed to amazingly long commutes or developed alternative sources of money. On the whole, though, most of the unattached stay in cities and grow accustomed to the crime rate, and bolt and bar the doors automatically, and plan after-dark excursions with care.

Wherever we live, our homes have one thing in common: a complex web of physical things to go wrong. Things to be coped with. I've heard that in some apartments in some cities a person called a superintendent comes running to fix whatever's broken, but I've never seen such a person myself. Sooner or later most of us have to come to grips with the machinery of our surroundings.

It's harder for those of us who were once married to reasonably competent men, or to men at least willing to give it a try. Talking to married women now, I'm impressed by the number of tasks they can shrug off. They say, "Oh, I'm hopeless with things like that," or "Bill understands the VCR, so I just let him do it." This is probably bad for their characters, a reassuring thought for us who must learn or go without. Maybe sometimes we can find a man to stop by and help; Diane, who has blue eyes and naturally curly hair, seems always to have a neighbor hurrying over to stop the toilet from gurgling or kick the balky pump in the basement. But most of us don't, or if we do, we find a man who hates to admit he doesn't know how to fix the pump so he does it anyway, and then later blue smoke comes pouring out of it and we still haven't learned anything.

It's crept up on us, this ignorance of our lives' machinery. Me, I'm afraid of electricity; my ex-husband was

quite masterful with it but afraid of gas: I re-lit the pilot light while he tinkered with the wiring. Now here I
sit surrounded by circuit breakers, fuse boxes, and
frayed plugs all leering ominously at me. It was only a
few months ago that I mustered the courage to rewire a
lamp. I had to get a book from the library and hold it
open the whole time, and it took me ages, but the lamp
works. I feel like patting it gratefully on the head whenever I pass.

I remember a minor crisis with the office toilet. It
refused to flush, throwing the married female staff into
panic and revulsion, as if graves had yawned and spewed
forth moldering bodies. I diagnosed it, and reported that
the rod to the flush handle had snapped, and all they had
to do was reach in and lift the stopper out of the hole by
hand.

The staff recoiled from me in horror: with their *hands?*
In the *tank*, I said. Not the bowl. Nobody pees in the
tank, it's water, as in tapwater.

They gave me looks that meant I was not just unfeminine but downright unwholesome. They used the next-
door office's toilet until a man, more resourceful and
kinder than I, rigged a coat hanger so they could flush
without touching tank water until the plumber came.

(I don't want to imply that ignorance is purely female. The following week my boss, a married man

and a father, hired a union carpenter to come with a screwdriver and tighten two screws on a loose door handle.)

It's consoling to know we can call professionals to come and do these things for us, but professionals are expensive, and they don't always hustle right over to help the minute we hang up the phone. One definition of eternity is the time it takes the locksmith to arrive after we've had our pocketbook snatched, complete with our address and keys.

It's bad for us to sit there waiting for him, too, sweating blood and listening for stealthy footsteps in the hall. Anything that makes us feel helpless is bad for us, and eats deeply into the brain centers we need in order to lead brave lives on our own. For the sake of sanity we must learn to take charge, to buy ourselves a decent hammer, not some ladylike toy, and a solid step stool so we can stop climbing on tables and windowsills. Much of what we haven't learned to do is surprisingly easy; much of it we would have learned simply by growing up as little boys instead of little girls, and taking an active, curious, destructive interest in how things work. It's not too late, though, to change our ways.

Take the matter of the lost or stolen door keys, or an ex-lover who calls to say he's coming to give you a piece of his mind, and you remember he still has a key.

He may arrive long before the locksmith, who in any case will charge you a hundred dollars or more, depending on where you live.

If you have a surface-mounted auxiliary lock—and you probably do if you live in the city—you can change it yourself in about seven minutes for under ten dollars. This is not the doorknob lock, which was basically designed to keep people from barging into the bathroom while you're shaving your legs; this is the serious lock fastened onto the door, with a drop-down or slide-over bolt, and it looks something like Figure 1. You'll need a screwdriver and two pairs of pliers.

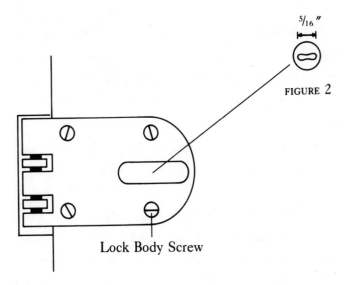

$^5/_{16}$ ″

FIGURE 2

Lock Body Screw

FIGURE 1

Take up the screwdriver and unscrew the body of the lock from the inside of the door. Turn it over and make sure it has a slot inside it that looks like Figure 2, which it probably does.

Find a neighbor to watch over your portable property and go to the hardware store or the hardware aisle of a general-goods chain store and buy what's called a replacement cylinder, with its own two keys. (I suppose the truly foresighted would already have one at home in a kitchen drawer.) You can carry your lock body with you for reassurance, and ask a salesperson, if there is one. If you don't have two pairs of pliers, supply yourself while you're there.

Come home and consider your door. With the lock body off, you're looking at the backing plate of the cylinder, which is also screwed on. (Figure 3 is the inside story.) Unscrew it. Go around to the other side of the door and take note whether the keyhole sits at the top or the bottom of its circle, then poke the cylinder on through to the outside and remove it. Now you have a hole in the door.

Break into the blister pack—this is the hardest part of the job—and take out your new cylinder. There's a tongue, or tab, that sticks out, which is the part that turns the bolt that keeps the burglars at bay. How long it should be depends on the thickness of your door, and this is why

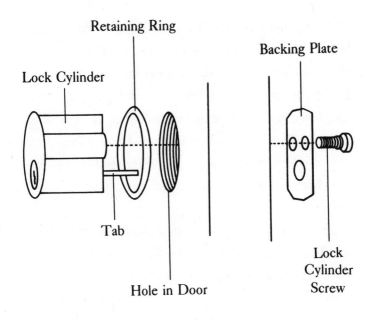

FIGURE 3

it's scored in places, so you can break it to the right length. Measure it against the tab on the old cylinder. If it's longer, mark which score line will shorten it to match and grab it with both your pliers, one on each side of the mark. Bend it firmly up and down until it breaks. (Be patient; it will.)

Slide the new cylinder into the hole in the door, with the keyhole at the top or bottom, depending on where the old one was. Your old backing plate will fit comfortably into its accustomed seat, so if it isn't bent, go ahead and use it, and its screws, and ignore the new ones. The tab will poke out through the largest hole. Insert the screws into the other holes by hand, then tighten them with the screwdriver while holding the cylinder in place from the outside. Before the final tightening, check to see that the keyhole sits straight up and down.

Put the lock body back on, making sure the tab fits into the slot inside it (Figure 2). Put the screws back in. If they feel loose and wobbly, pack the holes with toothpicks or kitchen matches or whatever's handy, then put the screws in and tighten them.

Now try the key. If it's hard to turn, loosen the screws again and move the lock body gently around while turning the key until you find the place where it turns smoothly. Then hold the lock body still while you tighten the screws again.

There you are, as safe as the Third Little Pig; the wolf will have to use the chimney. Take a friend out to dinner on the money you saved, leaving your earthly possessions secure at home.

Gradually, one at a time, I'm peeling back some of the mysteries and revealing the ordinary workings within them. Once in a while, I don't need to call a repairman.

I don't need to take the day off work and wait, and then when he finally arrives, watch him fix the wretched thing in five minutes and hand me a bill. The bill lists forty-five dollars for the house call, sixty-five for labor, and eighty-two cents for parts. Whimpering with gratitude, I pay it, and as he pockets the check on his way out he sneers over his shoulder, "Coulda done it yourself, lady. All you need's a screwdriver."

Respectfully, on tiptoe, I'm even approaching the dreaded electricity.

Electricity in a house or apartment is like a tree with branches. The main line coming into the building is the trunk, and branches reach out into different areas or appliances. They're left open or shut by fuses in older buildings and circuit breakers in newer ones. This is not for our greater confusion; it's for safety: if an area's overloaded or something's wrong, the fuse blows or the circuit breaker flips to shut off the power before the place explodes or burns down or whatever.

When a fuse blows or a circuit breaker flips, we have one of three problems. Either we're trying to suck more out of that circuit than it has to offer, such as plugging in a hair-dryer that was the last straw, or else the appliance itself—hair-dryer or whatever—has a problem, or else the problem lurks in the walls and needs an electrician.

Go look for the fuse box or the circuit box, usually in the basement or utility room and recognizable by its metal door. Open it. If it looks like Figure 4 it's a fuse box; Figure 5, it's a circuit-breaker panel. Do not be frightened; you can't fry just *looking* at it. Somebody should have labeled the fuses or switches with a diagram showing which areas and appliances go with which. If someone didn't, you can do it yourself by calling in a friend and

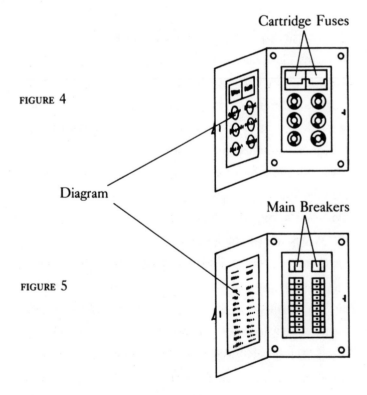

Cartridge Fuses

FIGURE 4

Diagram

Main Breakers

FIGURE 5

turning on all the lights and outlets and then turning off the switches or taking out the fuses, one by one, and having your friend yell which lights went off. Heavy users like an electric stove, clothes dryer, or air conditioner have their own private circuits, so if one of these flips or blows the trouble is in the appliance. Leave it off and call for help.

When a circuit-breaker switch flips, it's the one pointing in the "off" direction. Unplug or turn off everything in its area and flip the switch back to the "on" position. If it flips again, you have deep-seated troubles and need an electrician. If it stays on, start plugging things back in, starting with what has always been on that circuit. When you plug in the culprit the switch will flip off. Ask yourself: is this something new on this circuit? Unplug everything else again and try the new item, the hair-dryer or whatever, by itself. If the switch stays on, the hair-dryer's fine, you were just overloading that circuit; plug it into another room. But if the switch flips off with nothing else on the circuit, throw out the hair-dryer. Bury it deeply in the trash, so no passerby will pick it up, take it home, and flip a switch.

Fuses come in three types. Figure 6 is a plug type with a glass top and a copper screw base like a light bulb; Figure 7 is an S type with a ceramic screw base. The amp rating is on the bottom, and you must never

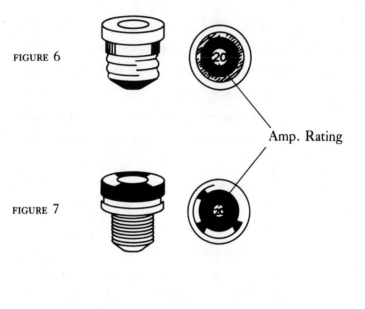

FIGURE 6

Amp. Rating

FIGURE 7

FIGURE 8

replace a smaller rating with a larger one. This under-protects the circuit, and you could start something you'd regret, like a fire. If it says 20, put in another 20. Figure 8 is a cartridge fuse for heavy appliances like stoves and, as mentioned, you don't replace it, you call the stove man.

Fuses are *not* hostile. (It may even be that electricity itself isn't hostile; I'm working on the concept.)

It's possible that, in our formative years, little girls were told to back off so they didn't get hurt while little boys were shown how fuses worked. Well, if we're going to live here with no boys around to help, I don't see why we have to sit in the dark. The last time I called an electrician he showed up in just under three weeks.

You don't need a rubber suit, just dry your hands before you set to work, don't stand in puddles, and have a flashlight if needed. How do you know which fuse blew? Inspect the nice new fuses you bought to keep on hand: that's what an unblown fuse looks like. A blown fuse looks cloudy or cracked inside, as if an explosion had happened, which it has. Check which area belongs to that fuse and follow the routine for circuit breakers. If, after you've unplugged everything and screwed in your new fuse, it blows, you're back to waiting for Sparky again, but at least you tried.

Trying strengthens the soul. It stiffens the sinews, summons up the blood, and leads us to take the lid off the toilet tank, flush, and watch closely what's supposed to happen, so we can help it happen when it doesn't. These are our homes, at least for the time being, and we need to take charge.

Some urban singles automatically move as soon as the lease is up, but this restless habit is probably bad for us. A lot of our mail and most of our magazines go astray, nobody, including us, remembers our new phone number, we have to reprint our business cards and résumés, and it's major stress. According to professionals in the stress-measuring business, moving ranks right behind divorce and a death in the family.

Maybe it's that first morning, in the gray before dawn when we open our eyes and see a window, a rectangle of lighter gray looking at us, and *it's in the wrong wall*. Solitary people have little enough to stabilize our centers of gravity without windows that slip around on us in the night.

Assuming we've found a reasonably livable place that hasn't yet put us in the poorhouse, we should try to stay in it. Put up with its shortcomings and try to make it feel like home, because we without families need homes. If we're bored, move the furniture around, have the couch re-covered, change the pictures on the walls. Work with what we've got.

Long ago when I was younger and certain things were still clear-cut, a single woman in my office took a course in carpentry and remodeled her apartment. She became a major, ongoing joke; if she'd taken up cigars, or football, she couldn't have been funnier. I'm grieved to report I went right along with the office majority and laughed too;

a woman who could build a handsome, functional window-seat storage cabinet was simply no woman at all. Well, *I* still couldn't, heaven knows, but my inadequacy doesn't seem such a virtue any more.

In our private quarters we can do anything we want, as long as we don't get caught keeping cats or hiring a rock band, and buy our own household goods to please nobody but ourselves. At a certain point, on one of those birthdays that keep rolling around, we can decide we're going to be here for a while and start replacing the battered makeshift furniture from thrift shops and family attics with things we want.

If we like them, and can eventually pay for them, we can have them, and there's no one to argue. No one matters here but us. Making a home for one's self doesn't have quite the righteous resonance of making a home for one's family, but it has the advantage common to all dictatorships: no arguments.

My ex-husband and I, within three months of our marriage, brushed close to the divorce courts twice, once over the matter of bedspreads and then again about a coffee table. Neither of us ever quite gave in. We were each convinced that we were deeply, inarguably right and that the other was not only wrong, ill-bred, and quite without taste but hatefully pigheaded about it too. Bedspread and coffee table smoldered under their own ashes for years.

Whatever sort of shelter we can find for ourselves, the worst thing about it is also the best thing: it's all ours.

Chapter 6

Food and Health

Dined alone, sad for want of company,
and not being very well, and know not
how to eat alone.

—SAMUEL PEPYS

Solitaries eat badly. As in other matters, we miss the modifying influence of family and, depending on our nature and metabolism, get fat from dining on cheesecake and chips or thin from not dining at all or peculiar from living on brown rice and cayenne pepper. Nobody says, "That's *dinner*? You've got to be kidding," or makes those familial privileged remarks about our new double chin.

Unlike people with families, we can eat anything we

want, and this ought to feel like a joyful freedom but most of the time it doesn't. Night after night after night we have to decide what to eat, find it, and eat it, all by ourselves. In the heart of a major city we can pick it up at the deli on the way home, a piece of cooked chicken and a plastic container of potato salad. We can send out for pizza, or won ton soup and the Buddhist's Delight. In the suburbs, if we're young and reckless, we can drive through the drive-through by the highway and take home a cheese-burger or a bucket of fried chicken. Everywhere, we can take our own leftovers or a frozen "entree" out of the freezer to be microwaved into edibility.

The microwave oven was supposed to save us, and it probably has improved the situation, since time is a factor in the problem. Even if we have absolutely nothing else to do, the idea of preheating a conventional oven and making it work for an hour just for our own personal din-ner seems, well, disproportionate. Fussing over our own food seems an unwarranted expenditure of spirit. Men feel aggrieved by the necessity; women suffer from the conviction that a proper woman should be feeding some-one else besides herself. It's our ancient role, all that gath-ering and pounding grain while the menfolk sat around sharpening their spears and painting themselves with berry juice. Who would pound grain for an hour and then sit down and eat it herself? Sharing food was basic to human civilization, its original underpinning, its glue, a first cause of our banding together so we could grow strong and numerous. The lone diner was always an outcast.

With the microwave, a frozen dinner that only machines have fussed with is ready to eat in six minutes or so, before we've lost interest in eating at all. A baking potato is edible in five to seven minutes, especially if you ignore the instructions to let it stand for two minutes, which most of us do. Maybe the texture isn't the same as when baked in a conventional oven, but we can't have everything.

The microwave has changed family life too. We sit here alone imagining a happy family gathered around the groaning board exchanging news of their days, but this has grown rare. Your basic happy family trails into the kitchen at any old hour, and even the youngest child can push the buttons to cook itself a frozen potpie, and here and there around the house they all change channels while they chew. We might as well be us.

Microwaves are fast. One executive single type I know says briskly that if dinner takes more than ten minutes to get itself ready, forget it. Ten minutes or she'll go without.

It may be—I don't have statistics—that a lot of us lone diners just don't get quite enough to eat. This is a peculiar thought in America, where it's taken for granted that most of us are fat or about to become so, a whole nation of us prowling the supermarket aisles in search of the "lite" and the "lo-cal," but it might be true. A recent study at Georgia State College, of all places, showed that the students put away 44 percent more food when they ate with friends than when they ate alone. That's a lot of food. Maybe we're hungry; maybe, after dining on the microwaved potato, hunger masked as gloom drives us to the midnight cheesecake eaten in the cold white light of the open refrigerator door.

We eat a lot of other people's food, food assembled by machines or strangers, brought home in frozen packets or pizza boxes. Maybe there's a psychological element we miss: the personal nourishment of food made just for us. Mother food. Maybe there's a vitamin, as yet unidentified, in meals put together by familiar hands, even if they're our own and not our mother's. Just in case, we should probably cook ourselves and perhaps our friends something from raw ingredients once or twice a week. Or we can cook a proper dinner for two and put half of it away on a plate to be microwaved tomorrow. If we don't eat it tomorrow, of course, we never will. Throw it in next week's garbage, plate and all.

It needn't be duck à l'orange. We can chop up some potatoes, slice an onion, slap on a chunk of butter, and microwave them till they're soft. Put them in the blender with some chicken broth. (We can do this more efficiently, I'm told, with a food processor, but many city kitchens simply cannot swallow another appliance, and some of us have to keep the blender on the floor and give away the toaster to make room for the microwave.) Blend them up, add some chives if you have them, and a good splash of cream and some more butter, and you have potato soup. Fast, bland, soothing, filling, nurturing. Packed with cholesterol. Theoretically it's possible to do the same thing with skim milk and nondairy butter, but psychologically it just wouldn't be the same.

We can spend Sunday afternoons cooking up a great pot of something the slow way, stew or chili or minestrone or chicken-and-noodles, and this has the advantage of not being *dinner*, exactly, but a creative pastime, like knitting sweaters, only sweaters don't smell as comforting. Then we can portion it out into microwavable plastic containers and put it in the freezer, where it stays, perhaps forever, or at least till we move to the next apartment. There's something bleak about a dozen containers of the same minestrone, sprouting frost and looking less and less edible as the weeks go by. Still, there it is in case you get snowed in.

I made an apple pie one Sunday. I make a very good apple pie, but nobody dropped in that week and it takes a single person over the age of twelve a long, long time to eat an apple pie. I hope I never see one again. I threw a lot of it away.

Single people waste enough food to feed a Third World country for a year. Our schedules are unstable. Friends call up with plans at the last minute, and what we were going to make for dinner sits in the refrigerator. The next day it has undergone some subtle change and no longer feels like the right thing to eat. For days after that we keep avoiding its reproachful eye every time we open the door, until it mutates into alien life-forms.

There's the supermarket panic, too. All we're looking for is something to feed ourselves, something for dinner, and the place is just too *big*. We can buy anything we want; we have no one to please but ourselves; but this freedom in the face of unlimited choices fills us with gloom and confusion. An hour later we come out with a jar of pickled oysters and a candy bar, having forgotten coffee and toilet paper, the real essentials of life. It helps a little to be desperately poor or on a severely restricted diet; these impose limits on choice and add the element of challenge. Various weight-loss plans offer us rigid menus or even provide a food or food-substitute; these may be popular because they lift the decision from our shoulders.

A journalist, newly widowed, wrote, "I'm mildly paranoid about my supermarket shopping cart. There's something exposed and forlorn about it, with its bottle of

Scotch, lone tomato, and twenty-four cans of Friskies for cats." At home, she had fifty-seven cookbooks, but since her husband's death her refrigerator had contained nothing but capers, mustard, and chutney.

People alone can fall into vile culinary ruts and, out of sloth and misery, stay there. One woman I know makes up weekly batches of chicken salad and lives on them, winter and summer, nourishing herself automatically in front of the television set. If it were possible to take the stuff intravenously she would.

I myself, during a rough patch of time, lived for weeks on hard-boiled eggs smeared with anchovy paste. It may have damaged my system permanently, and I don't remember liking them even in the beginning, but they seemed to strike a nice balance between starving to death and thinking up something else to eat. Besides, I could eat them standing up. If you don't sit down at the table, you don't have to face the fact that nobody's sitting there with you. Peel a hard-boiled egg and stand at the window eating it, watching all the people in the streets going home to their families with bags of groceries.

There are restaurants, of course, and they provide the lovely service of waiting on you, taking care of you, bringing you food with their own hands, and, in the better places, asking you constantly if you like it. Men living alone sometimes zero in on a convenient place and head for it automatically every night, greeting the waitperson by name and unfurling a newspaper as they sit down at the usual table.

They don't consider it fun, merely necessary. The husband alone in John Cheever's story, "Marito in Citta," pokes at his stringy pepper steak and orders ice cream so as not to hurt the waitress's feelings: "The food reminded him of all those who through clumsiness or bad luck must make their lives alone and eat this fare every night. It was frightening, and he went to a movie . . ."

You see fewer women than men dining alone in public. Perhaps we feel guiltier about paying others to feed us; perhaps fewer of us can afford it. Perhaps we feel itchy and conspicuous, alone in plain sight. Women with resident men at home tell us that walking into a restaurant alone must be the most daunting experience a solitary woman faces. It isn't. Plenty of things are much more daunting and don't get any less so with practice, but with very little practice you can learn to love your neighborhood restaurant so well all your credit cards turn red and start blinking.

It's permissible in the beginning, if you feel self-conscious, to bring a small book with you, but I don't recommend newspapers. Reading the paper in crowded quarters like restaurants and commuter trains is a sex-linked talent; men manage so deftly, but most women will knock over their wineglass and bloody their neighbor's nose trying to turn the page. With a book as a blind, you can get some good eavesdropping done. A lone female, unless she's stark naked or blindingly beautiful or famous, is invisible and allowed to overhear juicy gossip. I once listened to a confession of murder; it didn't seem to be a joke.

Wherever we eat, we should try to enjoy it. It ought to be one of life's pleasures, and ignoring what we chew while reading or watching television deprives us of part of the range of good things available. Liking food isn't a very American concept, unfortunately. Thoreau thought it was as "impure" to eat "sensually" as to cohabit, which is pretty impure. He said, "Not that food which entereth into the mouth defileth a man, but the appetite with which it is eaten. It is neither the quality nor the quantity, but the devotion to sensual savors . . . food for the worms that possess us . . . The wonder is how they, how you and I, can live this slimy beastly life, eating and drinking."

The wonder, really, isn't that Thoreau lived in the woods for two years, but that people ever let him come back out.

In Europe, food is expected to taste good. Even the bread tastes good. In America, we don't seem to expect to enjoy eating; apparently we're willing to eat almost anything labeled and advertised as food. Depending on our age and social status, we eat things simply because they're there, like hamburgers, or because the lower classes haven't heard of them yet or wouldn't touch them with a barge pole, like radicchio and sushi, or because the food police recommend them as the one safe thing this week.

The food police have made it harder to eat alone. The simple comforting supper of scrambled eggs and bacon and buttered toast, or maybe a cheese omelet, quickly tossed together, the ingredients always on hand, might as well be paint-stripper with a side of ground glass. The easy lamb chop, the cold fried chicken from yesterday, the bowl of potato salad, the glass of milk: poisoners all, and the cheerful friendly apple has been sprayed with whatever her stepmother put on Snow White's.

They keep changing the rules too. We have to stay alert, and read the papers daily to update our food phobias. For a decade broccoli was everywhere; it prevented cancer, and was served in restaurants whether you asked for it or not. Then we were told that, while we had to go on eating it, we should wash it in hot water and detergent first. Last year a mysterious oil in seafood conferred immortality; this year the fish are full of PCBs and the oysters have hepatitis. Up until recently, oat bran unclogged our arteries, and the virtuous chewed their way through sacks of horse-feed until word came out that its only advantage was that while they were chewing it, they weren't eating french fries, which are said to be worse, at least this week.

To make matters more difficult, the watchdogs keep coming up with food that causes one disease while preventing another; we have to juggle the trade-offs. For years anxious people avoided real coffee because it caused heart attacks and high blood pressure and ulcers and coffee nerves. They greeted the day with various hot brown waters instead, until a new study came out showing that coffee much improves the sex life, especially among those older folk whose sex lives might need help. Choose: ulcers or impotence? The drinking of alcoholic beverages has been held for a decade to be suicidal, and all the right people switched to bottles of French or Italian water. Now they tell us that a couple of drinks a day may help prevent heart attacks—while still doing all those awful *other* things, of course—and the bottles of water are full of sodium, which is something else we should worry about.

In the seventies an earnest and vocal group believed we'd all be saved from hell by switching to honey instead of sugar; one faction even believed sugar caused crime waves. Nowadays sugar is one of the few things we're allowed to eat, along with carbohydrates, the dreaded "starchy foods" of yesteryear. Keeping up with the news from the food front is challenging.

For those who feel this adds excitement to the supermarket trip, narrowing the choices as we steer our carts through the wilderness of poisons, there's nothing wrong with it as long as we don't get wildly carried away. The rest of us might as well ignore the whole thing.

After all, here we are picking our lone paths across the abyss, with plenty of real things to worry about, like losing our jobs or our wallets or falling in love with the Boston Strangler, or even just falling down the stairs; do we really have time to be frightened of our food? We're omnivores. We were designed to eat pretty much everything we can chew except grass and that which runs faster than we do, and omnivorous is a good thing to be. It broadens our experience and protects against disasters like the oat bran crop failing; we can go back to the brown rice of twenty years ago. Or lamb chops. Besides, the more things we aren't allowed to eat, the more we have to eat the few permissible items, and they may have problems of their own. Half the people I know have sworn off red meat and many of them now are dodging all that contaminated fish. They eat chicken every night. They have a book called *365 Ways to Cook Chicken*, the most depressing title I can imagine staring at in the kitchen. Chicken, I hear, is stuffed with hormones and antibiotics and heaven knows what other medicinal substances, affecting us heaven knows how.

The fear of food makes it harder to shop for our solitary meals. Just reading all those labels, as we're urged to do, checking for fats and sodium and wondering what "hydrogenated" means, takes the bloom off dining. Surely finding something for dinner tonight is a more immediate problem than the future of our arteries. (Yes, I know arteries are too serious to take lightly in America. In France, *livers* are too serious to take lightly.)

Like other crotchets, an obsession with personal health can take root and flourish in solitary folk. Nothing, no one, prevents us or laughs at us when we get up at six in the morning in a blizzard and run three miles. Presently maintaining the status quo fails to give us that thrill of achievement and we up the ante. We go out at five in the morning and run ten miles. We live on lettuce and cereal; we run all night.

Most of us, mercifully, get bored with the whole thing and go back to bed where we belong, but plenty of addicts out there are slipping over the edge. I know a man who eats absolutely nothing, ever, even in the homes of friends, except plain boiled pasta and steamed broccoli. He runs, too. He's getting a bit cadaverous, almost skeletal, but he claims to feel great. There's a funny glitter in his eye, though. Sometimes the line between fitness and madness seems to be thinning.

One of the advantages of coronary health is the chance to brag about it. You can't get away with it on any other subject. Brag about your cleverness or your bank account and your audience will give you the raspberry, as well they should, but the health types can buttonhole total strangers and tell them for hours how they brought their cholesterol down through boring food and running around in the dark like thieves. The strangers listen patiently, waiting for the chance to talk about their own pulse rates and their own cholesterol.

Health hasn't done much for the level of general conversation, since the drama of it doesn't extend much beyond the limits of the owner's skin. I keep hoping it will go away, but it doesn't. Perhaps it's permanent. Perhaps America has found her true expression, the shape of her full flowering, not as a great intellectual or epicurean or spiritual culture, but as a purely physical society dedicated to the personal fitness of the individual. Even more than the sex craze that preceded it, fitness has spawned a lot of business; gyms, health clubs, diet supplements, special garments for various exercises; the shoe wardrobe alone is a formidable industry. Sports medicine, formerly the arcane corner of a handful of doctors in charge of doping up wounded football players so they could keep on playing, has proliferated to treat the knees, feet, and tendons of the health-minded. Hideous machines have sprouted in our homes, so we can pretend to be rowing a boat in the living room. My brother keeps a sort of metal giraffe in the guest room; if he used it, it would simulate cross-country skiing, but he apparently keeps it for the sole purpose of maiming unwary guests in the dark.

In the olden days, when we felt poorly our friends recommended rest, sleep, nourishing food, perhaps a week in the islands. Now we should do ten extra sit-ups. If we're tired and sleepy we should run farther; sleep is now actually *bad* for us, since our muscles start to waste away almost before our heads hit the pillow.

All in all, an exhausting hobby. And, as mentioned earlier, far more dangerous to the solitary, since we don't have families to worry about or family errands to run or spouses to tell us to cut it out and come to bed. We're at liberty to spend endless hours brooding about our health. Wondering what's safe to eat, which shoes to run in.

I have nothing against health in moderation, but taken to extremes it's isolating, and we're isolated enough already. It affects no one but our personal selves; we aren't saving the world, or even saving the whales, and who, pray tell, has time to do it if not those without families to save? Besides, health is lonelier than sex; back in the sex days, at least two bodies were involved.

Ultimately, too, health and fitness are bound to be disappointing, since the object is to live forever and never get sick. Nobody is angrier, nobody feels more bitterly cheated, than the serious health person coming down with flu. Ambient viruses, billowing through the office corridors in March, don't seem to care how many foods you quit eating or how far you pretended to row.

Slothful or vigorous, carnivore or vegetarian, sooner or later we're going to get sick. Living alone, we get sick alone. There's no one to take care of us or bring us some soup, and sometimes, if we're running a fever and feeling a bit light-headed to begin with, this can seem dreadfully sad.

It isn't really. Very few invalids get taken care of any more. Small children, maybe, but often by a sitter, at least after the first day or two, since mommy's office can't live without her. Even married men, once deliciously pampered and their fevered pillows plumped up, now find themselves grumbling around alone in the kitchen warming their own soup. The family woman has rarely ever been able to take to her bed; she has always tottered through the house nursing the rest of the family, all of whom claim to be equally ill. Even if they aren't ill, they feel obscurely threatened by her sickness and retaliate by making messes and fabricating crises. Sick family women should go to the hospital. Alone, at least we can go to bed.

Keep a supply of soup and tea on hand. Keep over-the-counter medicines in abundance, so you don't have to bundle up in scarves and trudge off to the drugstore. Of course, it's illegal to have a broad-spectrum antibiotic on hand for the next time bronchitis rears its horrible head, and I'd be the last person in the world to suggest that, instead of finishing up the prescription as you were told to do, you save two or three in case it strikes again on a Saturday night, and it's snowing, and there wouldn't be any taxis even if your doctor were available, which he isn't. Swallowing an antibiotic pill without first going out in the bitter east wind and then sitting around in a doctor's waiting room enveloped in even more exotic germs is against the law, and don't say I didn't say so. However, we *are* allowed to keep aspirin and its relatives, Kaopectate, Pepto-Bismol, decongestants, Ace bandages, Robitussin, and such-like minor remedies, and we should. Friends may rush to our side with food and medicine, or then again, they may have their own agendas.

My gentle doctor held my wrist absent-mindedly between thumb and fingers and frowned and said, "I'd like to put you in the hospital. I really would. A severe bronchitic condition like that, and no one to take care of you . . ."

"People will take care of me," I said bravely, and coughed. "Everyone will take care of me."

David brought me a bag of groceries but he couldn't stay; he had to go spend the weekend with his parents. Elaine ran over with a bottle of Scotch but she couldn't stay; she had house guests.

Carol was out, and I thought about leaving a message on her answering machine and then didn't, and hung up. Emily had gone to the country. Tom was in Scotland.

What could they do for me anyway; what did I need from them? Someone to sit in a chair and look at me while I coughed? Someone to feel my fevered brow and read me a story? Visiting the sick was once a recognized charitable occupation for underemployed women and conscientious clergymen, but the custom seems to be fading. Why visit the sick anyway? They're usually lousy company and often contagious. I had been to the doctor; I had filled the prescription; I would get well alone.

I took my pills and coughed and coughed.

Saturday morning was sunny and warmer. The sun from the east windows lay clear across the floor. Then retreated to the edge of the rug. Across the rug. Off the end of the couch. Then sucked itself up the side of the radiator, and it was noon.

I sat on the couch and read a novel all the way through, stopping only to cough and take pills. The well-stocked treatment center should also include, somewhere between the vitamin C and the toothache drops, a fresh, unopened novel and an unplayed videotape, something with a chase scene and pratfalls to tempt the listless attention.

Around four, the sun came in briefly from the north, bounced off someone else's windows. From the couch I could see the house across the street, and the shadow thrown by its dormer. The shadow got longer and longer, and then was swallowed up by general shadow and it was evening.

I warmed up some soup, but by the time it was hot I'd lost interest in it and drank some Scotch instead. There was nothing exciting on television, or nothing exciting enough. I coughed for a while and went to bed. The streetlight outside, unlike the sun, was stationary and made the same square on the wall all night, whenever I woke up to cough.

In the morning I felt better. Sooner or later we usually do.

Being sick alone just isn't all that much more dangerous than being sick surrounded by loved ones. It's just lonelier. In times of physical helplessness a voice in all of us cries "Moth-*err*!" Wounded soldiers on the battlefield call for mother. So do people who live alone and find themselves with flu. We want someone to say, "Are your feet warm enough?" or "Let me feel your forehead" or "Did you get something to eat?" Someone to take the intense personal interest in our physical condition that no one else ever has or ever will, and that probably irritated us into tantrums, back in the days of being mothered.

There's nothing to be done except shoulder her job as best we can; get a flu shot in November; sleep as long as possible; walk around in what used to be called the fresh air for exercise; resign ourselves sensibly when we do get sick. And, of course, keep feeding ourselves.

Inevitably, dinner time rolls around.

"Everyone's lonely," said Ann, over lunch. It was February and raining. "I have a million friends and they all say they're lonely. My bridge group, my tennis friends, everyone. Even the *men* are lonely." We looked out the window for a while at darkness and umbrellas. "I think I could handle it," she said, "if I just didn't have to eat dinner alone every night."

Millions and millions of us, every night. When so many people have the same problem, it seems that there must be a solution somewhere, a better way. Could we set up feeding centers somehow; something midway between a friend's house and a restaurant? Something like the London clubs in English novels? Read Evelyn Waugh;

read P. G. Wodehouse—no lonely dinners for Jeeves's Bertie. Nightly, Jeeves handed him his hat and he popped around to the Drones Club where, at the bar, he found someone to go into the dining room with him. Where are the sociable supper clubs for our solitaries? Places of nourishing food and easy, unplanned company, whatever the hour, since some of us work unpredictably late. Friendly faces instead of Dan Rather while we chew. I don't know how we'd set them up, or pay the rent, or afford the kitchen staff, since volunteers with day jobs are unreliable. Still, there must be a better way than this.

Nightly, we all have to stand in the same spot, sometime between six and ten, staring sadly into the freezer and wondering why those little boxed dinners all taste of box and why, after we've eaten them, we don't seem to have eaten at all. Opening the wire-handled container from the deli, slowly, because when we were children we brought home goldfish in containers just like this and it's possible that when we lift the flaps we'll find, not pasta salad, but an orange fish floating belly-up in a plastic bag of water.

Until we figure out the better way to eat, I submit a few suggestions, food to make for ourselves when the occasion calls for them. None of these have been approved by the American Heart Association, Weight Watchers, or the food police.

For October, when the days are getting shorter and your coat smells of mothballs:

BAKED APPLE: Cut the top off a large apple and dig out the core. Drop a pat of butter in the hole; sprinkle with nutmeg, cinnamon, and sugar. Microwave four minutes. Or, since it smells better that way and warms up the kitchen, bake in a real oven at 350 degrees for thirty minutes to an hour, depending on the apple's size and density.

For after Christmas shopping, when your feet got wet and you couldn't find anything you were looking for:

CIDER & RUM: Heat a cup of apple cider with broken bits of cinnamon stick and a couple of cloves. Let simmer; change into bedroom slippers. Pour through strainer into a mug heated with hot water. Add a dollop of butter and a shot of rum or brandy.

On a gray winter Sunday after the holidays, with nothing to do:

TAMALE PIE: In a big heavy frying pan, cook chopped onions and garlic till they're soft; add a pound or less of ground beef, break it up and cook it till it isn't pink. Sprinkle with cumin and chili powder and cook some more. Add a small can of tomato sauce and a can of tomatoes, chopped. Cook this down a bit and add a splash of salsa; the more depressed you are, the more salsa will be needed. While this simmers, mix a cup of yellow cornmeal with half a cup of cold water and add it to two and a half cups of boiling water. Cook ten minutes or so, stirring with a long-handled wooden spoon. In a casserole, spread the cornmeal on the bottom and layer on up with the meat-and-tomato mix, ending with decorative scoops of cornmeal. Bake for half an hour or so in a 350-degree oven. The cornmeal part is soothing and motherly; the fiery part stimulates the appetite and promotes courage. The quantity is generous—you can invite a friend over, or keep reheating it in the microwave for days, eliminating the need to make decisions.

For severe depression and occasions of grief and loss:

NO DINNER: Bring home a bag full of apples, nuts, cheese, crackers, grapes, oatmeal cookies, muffins, and popcorn. Put these out in bowls here and there, anywhere except where you usually sit down to eat. Pick at in passing.

For anxiety, insomnia, and fits of loneliness:

FETTUCINE WITH CALORIES: Cook and drain half a pound of fettucine. Sauté several chopped scallions in butter, stir in a cup of chicken broth, and boil for several minutes. Take the pan off the heat and slowly stir in a half cup of heavy cream. Add the fettucine, a cup of sour cream, a quarter of a cup of grated Parmesan, and some chopped chives if you have them. Mix.

For August, when you're tired of eating:

CUCUMBER SOUP: Before you go to work in the morning, peel and chop two cucumbers and slice a couple of scallions. Chop a quarter of a cup or so of fresh dill. Put about half the cucumbers, the onions, the dill, a dash of minced—not powdered—garlic, salt, pepper, and half a cup of plain yogurt in the blender or food processor and whirl it till smooth. Pour it into a bowl and stir in the rest of the cucumbers and another cup and a half of yogurt. Put it in the refrigerator and go to work. This will be enough for tonight and tomorrow too.

KIDNEY BEANS: A can of the best available kidney beans from the refrigerator, sprinkled with parsley and perhaps some garlic. Serve with a bowl of lettuce leaves, to be eaten with the fingers. Both these items need salt, I don't care what anyone says.

My grandmother's cough mixture:

Equal parts of honey, whiskey, and fresh lemon juice. Stir often. Sip. There are those who would consider this mixed jolt of sugar and alcohol practically life-threatening, though heaven knows what's in the potions they buy at the drugstore. Anyway, it's grandmotherly, for times when we need a grandmother.

Chapter 7

Work

Blessed is he who has found his work;
let him ask no other blessedness.

—THOMAS CARLYLE

Almost all of us have to work, and this is right and proper. Boring, exhausting, repetitive, or underpaid as our jobs may be, we must rise and dress in the morning, travel to them, speak to the people there, and go to bed at night before three in order to rise and dress again the next day. Without jobs, we could get into serious trouble. Jobs keep our lives in order and our souls in touch.

I do know some solitary folk who don't need to work,

and don't. Four of them, to be exact, all men. (There was a woman, but she died of boredom.) None of them is really rich, which would make a difference, but they all have enough money to live on, enough to make working seem pointless, so that if they do take jobs they almost immediately get restless and quit, or argue with the boss and get fired. Of course, if they had much more money they probably wouldn't be alone, ever, except in the bathroom with the door locked. They'd have town houses in London, A-frames on the ski slopes, and villas in the south of France, with company climbing in through every window.

Three out of my four are or have recently been dangerously heavy drinkers. They sleep late, and are rarely seen on the streets before noon. One of them has developed such eccentric hours that his friends have almost given up trying to connect with him; at lunch time he's still asleep, and by dinner time his thoughts are on toast and coffee. By night, alone, he prowls and putters through stacks of books and half-finished canvases, painting, reading a few pages here, a few pages there. With a talent for puttering, my unemployed friends can fill the hours tolerably well until Happy Hour. It's amazing how long it can take to read the newspaper if you don't skip a single word, and reading the paper, even the columns of used motorcycles for sale, feels brisk and businesslike.

For them, time is the enemy. One claims to need, for sheer survival, ten to twelve hours of sleep. One keeps deciding to get a master's degree, and starts courses; then something goes wrong, the professor's a fool, the outside reading is dull, the hour is inconvenient. One has joined literally everything joinable in the city, and goes to the business meetings of obscure little museums on side streets and to dinners where librarians are awarded certificates of merit.

They're drowning in time, choking on it. When they wake up in the afternoon it lies on their faces like an extra pillow. They have to climb up through it every day by means of tiny tasks and habits and worries, like climbing a spiderweb. To the employed, their concerns seem hilarious. Is the cleaning woman sneaking sherry? Shall I confront her with it? But suppose I'm wrong, suppose she isn't? How embarrassing. Easier maybe just to fire her without mentioning sherry. After all, how can I feel comfortable having her around when I'm not sure she's honest? I couldn't sleep a wink last night.

Shall I serve fajitas? I served quiche the last time. Shall I trade in the concert ticket for another night? Call her back, or wait for her to call me?

For the rest of us, the daily waters are often cold and angry and sometimes dangerous; for the comfortably independent loners they're warm and sticky and thick as soup. We envy them, and wonder why they don't do all the exciting, useful, challenging things we're sure *we'd* do if we didn't have to work, but they don't, somehow. Struggling through the hours has sapped their strength.

Let's rejoice, then, in this mixed blessing, the jobs we do because we need the money.

Ah, yes. Money. The past decade has been confusing on the subject. As the financial scandals of the 1980s unfolded in the early nineties, self-righteous editorializers who hadn't cashed in began to refer to the "Greed Decade," and the people who had cashed in tried to lower their profiles. Not surprisingly, the newly superrich were almost all men; it was a shock, perhaps an invigorating shock, to find a highly visible, indictable woman misbehaving with money. Perhaps the times really have been changing.

Men with seven-figure incomes are now trying to keep out of the news, but women are still being urged to get rich—legally, if possible—by advertisers of expensive goods and services. Supported by these merchants, magazines have sprung up to show us a gallery of high-income role models. Their glossy pages introduce us to the lady whose taxes for a year are more than our salaries for five. We read how gallantly she struggles to snatch time for her toddler from her job as a Wall Street trader or CEO of a Fortune 500 company; how she dresses simply and plainly in thousand-dollar skirts and blouses; how she copes with stress by means of her exercise program and quick visits to her simple country place. Numerically, these women are all but nonexistent, but some magazines are devoted entirely to them; the editors may or may not be inventing them, using hired models. Certainly *I* never meet any of them, though of course they wouldn't have time to meet anyone. Readers are encouraged to feel that, since these paragons are the only working women mentioned, we alone are still shopping for bargains, and we have only ourselves to blame. We have missed the shower of gold in the eighties and landed unrich and bewildered in the nineties, still making the same old two thirds of a man's salary, still not stockbrokers or brain surgeons.

Some of the problem really is our fault. Our ambitions are flawed. We aren't trying hard enough, or caring fiercely enough or consistently enough. We may have struggled valiantly for the degree and competed successfully for the first job, and then lost momentum, to find ourselves floating among the orange peels in the wake of the prosperity boat. We may have been too nice.

Unmarried and female, if we're not nice to the world out there, what will it do to us? If we make it angry, how shall we defend ourselves?

Many women, including those young enough to know better, plus quite a lot of men in positions of power, secretly subscribe to the old ethic, as follows: (*a*) women are fed and housed by their husbands and fathers, and work only for money to buy clothes they don't really need; (*b*) a woman in a responsible job is taking that job away from a man, who has a family and really needs it; and (*c*) a woman who wants to work should give piano lessons, discreetly, in her own home, but if she must go out and work in public—maybe she doesn't own a piano—she should work in a job of direct service to men or small children, since this is the right and natural way of things. Some fanatics even believe it's biblically ordained. It may be another generation before this conviction fades completely from the subconscious—and from the structural underpinnings of corporations, where it's built into the bricks and mortar.

It's hard enough coping with this nonsense from bosses and corporations, and when we privately agree with them it can do us even more damage. It can keep the vast faceless armies of us making life more convenient for the men we work for, and being badly paid because we're basically the wife at work, and who pays wives? When women and typewriters moved into the office a hundred years ago, the family structure moved in with them.

From the moment typewriters stopped being experimental machinery and became practical, it was clear that typing was woman's work; helpful, wifely, badly paid, and unsuitable for men. Male journalists and authors were careful never to use more than two fingers, and bragged about it; the journalists then took to using the telephone instead and the authors struck it rich and hired secretaries who took dictation. A man who could type with ten fingers was like a man who knitted his own sweaters, while a woman who typed with two fingers was unemployable.

Until quite recently, many companies had a standing rule that any female job applicant, no matter what her degrees or qualifications or prospective position, had to take a typing test. She could not be considered without it, and the results went into her permanent file. Inexperienced men were hired with the assumption that they would be trained in their jobs; women had to arrive with "skills," and typing was the first and most basic of these. Filing, or the ability to remember the alphabet, was the second. Shorthand was of a higher order, and placed the applicant in a different and better-paid category; at the ultimate pinnacle of her career, in fact. She might be only twenty, but she had reached the top, or secretarial, rung.

Some offices might also require a woman to add up a column of figures or work a switchboard. These four or five accomplishments comprised a woman's career. It was taken for granted that no man in the office, no matter what the emergency might be, could do what she did, any more than he could have a baby. Traditionally, women haven't been well paid for having babies, either; it's something they should *want* to do, gladly, freely, for personal fulfillment. Support work in the office has always had the same aura. A man whose devoted longtime secretary demanded a raise was hurt as personally as if his dog had asked for paid vacations, and a clever secretary would couch the request as a matter of need rather than entitlement, so the boss could offer it to her out of the kindness of his heart. The office was indeed like one big happy family.

In the seventies, when computers began to move into the office, they were expected to change the image. After all, computers were serious science, and expensive too, and the women at their keyboards would be serious employees and paid as such.

We all know what happened to that notion. So many women flooded in to sit at the keyboards that the computer itself underwent a mysterious chemical change, and was seen one morning not to be serious or scientific at all but just another typewriter. Back to square one.

A single woman in a support job—research assistant, administrative aide, whatever—is in serious danger of liking the status quo, especially if the boss is male and a decent chap. If he's an ungrateful hound she'll divorce him for a different boss, but if he worries about her illnesses, compliments her work, notices her clothes, and says, "God, what would I do without you?" she may spend her entire working life at half-pay serving him gladly. Unless, of course, after ten years he announces one afternoon that he's accepted a better offer in Houston and Friday is his last day. This is a shattering blow comparable to the nastiest divorce. Worse, maybe, since not only is he leaving her after all these years without a backward glance, but she's forced to realize that she was lying to herself all along. It meant nothing. He never cared about her personally, any more than he cared for his telephone or his desk chair. The bread she was living on turns to ashes, and has always been ashes, and she has been a fool. An underpaid fool.

For millennia women have worked for love instead of money, and if we love our sweet boss, how can we ask for money too? How can we walk out and leave him, all helpless as he'd be without us, just because someone else has offered us more? Only a tramp, a slut, would leave a man because another man offered more money.

It seems ludicrous, in the light of those magazine women who battled their way to six figures, that so many of us are still dragging love and service and family feelings into the workplace like gum on our shoes, but we are. How can we help it? We may have a perfectly nice cat at home and dozens of wonderful friends, maybe a lover, but the office is where we spend our forty or more weekly working hours, and office relationships come to mean too much. Even without the adored boss, our work-friends can feel like family, and what would we do without them? What other family do we have?

According to Gloria Steinem, founding mother of feminism, the average secretary is better educated than her boss by a year and a half. So why is this woman placing this man's phone calls for him? Whose fault is it? Not his, surely; we can hardly expect him to insist on trading desks and salaries with her. Are we scared of his desk? Of money? Of power? Sure, why not? Think of the hostility power would bring down on our heads, and how people would hate us, and envy us, and conspire for our jobs, and stab us in the back. We're all alone here; can we handle that?

We weren't brought up to fight for power. Girl children, in these enlightened days, are encouraged to excel, go for the advanced degree and get out there and have interesting jobs. Girl children are rarely told to grow up competing for money and power. Boy children rarely need to be told. It's old-fashioned to believe in basic chemical gender differences, but anyone who has raised children— or puppies or kittens—of both sexes believes it anyway. And regardless of what our parents say, every girl learns on the playground not to make male enemies. An angry little boy can knock down a little girl and rub dirt in her eyes and throw her books in a puddle and there's very little she can do about it, except get another boy to spring to her defense. Is she going to grow up to compete fiercely for this angry boy's job, especially if no man stands beside her?

A recent survey showed that married women were more often promoted to responsible jobs than single ones. The conclusion was that being married was seen by employers as an asset, but it may mean, instead, that women with husbands feel safer battling their way up.

We need to be nice. Carlyle said, "No man lives without jostling and being jostled; in all ways he has to elbow himself through the world, giving and receiving offense." Offense? Us? Having searched for the right toothpaste and the guaranteed deodorant, we're to go out and give offense on purpose?

There are courses we can take on giving offense; assertiveness, it's called. Standing up for our rights against people who don't think we have any. Typically, according to psychiatrists, these lessons give us a temporary high, and for days or weeks we're king, and then we fall. The magic vanishes. We barge in and ask for a raise and the boss throws us out of the office without even glancing up from his work. We insist on certain rights from our lover, and he packs his toothbrush and never speaks to us again.

We're worse off than before and far more wormy in our mind's eye, because it's more depressing to have tried and failed than never to have tried at all.

Interesting jobs, yes; competitive striving, no. Let us all be ballerinas, painters, novelists, sopranos, and even gorilla-watchers, as long as no man wants our places in the world. Let us hope to work in fields where no one makes much money, or minds about it, because the job is so interesting and money is so dangerous.

Millions of women fought like tigers against the Equal Rights Amendment, as if it were trying to push us off a cliff into the yawning dark below.

A friend, divorced, with her own business, said, "I was brought up to believe if I worked hard I'd be a success, and I have worked hard, and I guess I'm pretty successful. But there's never the pressure a man has. I always knew that if I failed, no one would think the worse of me." She considered, and added, "Some people would like me more."

I have stared deeply into my soul, and there's a salary barrier in there, clumsily adjusted upward for inflation as the years go by. Above that mark I'd be a stranger to myself, different, hard, greedy, soulless, capable of firing a man with three kids and tears in his eyes. Incomprehensible things would be expected of me; the pilot would hand me the controls of the plane and drop dead.

And always, of course, there's the matter of the prince.

When they make you head of Research and Development, and you tell that engineer, the one with the deep voice and the eyelashes, just what's the matter with his cost-per-unit projection and how fast he'd better refigure it, he won't reply by asking you to dinner. Maybe he should; maybe in some golden future he will, but not today. Some things haven't changed. For romance, in the career structure, men look on the rungs below and women on the rungs above, and the higher we rise the fewer princes we'll find overhead. We needn't even be climbing the same ladder, just making more money. Holding more advanced degrees. The prince wants Cinderella, not the queen.

Men seem to drink in competitiveness with their Gerber's apple juice, and they aren't likely to fall in love with a woman who's already outrun them. Men and women feel differently about money. Women see it as a means to an end: invest it and we'll feel safer; spend it and we'll have nicer clothes, a sunnier apartment. Men see it as the measure of their worth, a kind of penis extension, and compare it to other men's money. My friend Steve hates not only his job but his whole field; hating it poisons his days. He's stuck with it, though, probably forever, because changing would mean making less money. He makes three times what I make and has only himself and a very small dog to spend it on; earning less would hardly affect the way he lives. It would affect the way he feels about himself, though. He'd be shorter. Smaller. Less.

Certainly a lot of men would be happier if they could take their salaries more lightly. Certainly a lot of women would be richer if they could take them more seriously.

Those of us who were once married are carrying a double burden in the matter. If we worked back then, we were a two-income family, but the way we lived was held to reflect our husband's job, not ours. Ideally, our income was a kind of private supplement, maybe earmarked for school tuitions and summer camps, maybe spent on such temporary, easily forgotten amenities as food, day care, and vacations, while our husband's firm, solid, masculine contribution was invested in the house and car. At dinner parties, we refrained from talking about our jobs, our raise, or the new account we'd landed; in the bedroom we did not bore our husbands with details of our working day. In many such households, the wife's job is seen mainly as the nuisance around which the day's chores must be arranged. The hard facts of her money can blur in her own mind, and the whole enterprise takes on a flimsiness, an unreality, like a dream someone told her about. Her job simply doesn't matter, not the way her husband's job matters.

After this, small wonder the widowed and divorced

don't march in and insist on a transfer and promotion. Small wonder we're grateful to stretch out our salaries to cover the rent, patching holes as we go, like piecrust.

Many of us are in the jobs we're in quite by accident, as if we'd fallen down an abandoned well and decided to set up a desk and chair in it. It was the first thing that offered itself, or we couldn't afford law school, or we knew someone who had a friend there, or we'd run away from home. Most often, we didn't have our eye on the ball at the time. Gazing into the future, we didn't see ourselves as biologists or pediatricians, and take steps toward that end. We saw that damned prince again. *He* looked like an end, heaven knows why. This seems to be almost as severe a problem now as it was thirty years ago, though more women are surviving it now, pulling their grade-point averages back up and paying attention again. Very few young men, then or now, have ever dumped their future careers without a second thought because they fell in love at twenty-two; it's a female problem.

Some of us, in spite of the pitfalls, do have great jobs and are, as Carlyle said, blessed. The rest of us should take stock. Alone, without families, or with children finally in all-day schools, our jobs are our social and worldly reality, our connection to the wheels that move things forward, and a major source of nourishment. We need to deal with them bravely; maybe even take a risk for a change. A woman with a two-year-old and a husband who wants his dinner at six looks for easy work, with regular or flexible hours, because her working day is less than half her work. Alone, we can look for something tougher. Stick our necks out. Spend more time. Exercise our courage, which seems to be a kind of muscle and subject to softening; too many years in that kindly office with the gentle boss and we can barely lift a pencil with it. The rest of the world begins to look like a nest of vipers. If we do run into competition that plays hardball, we cave in without a fight and run for our lives.

We haven't been properly programmed for taking chances. We don't invent something beautifully simple like the Frisbee or the hanging file, patent it, invest our friends' last cent, market it, slit the competition's throat and make a fortune. If we strike oil in the flower bed, we look around for some man to sell the rights to for fifty dollars, because what do we know about oil? The boldest entrepreneurs among us have opened needlework shops or they're making carrot cake and watercress sandwiches as a penny-ante catering service for the neighbors and barely breaking even; they use real cream in everything and don't charge half enough.

Looking at the glossy success of those women in magazines, most of us don't think, If she can do it, so can I. We think of her as an alien. Only marginally human, and scarcely female at all. Certainly a bitch. Not nice like us. Our boss would *hate* her. (Not, of course, that she'd care.)

It's time we brought a little grit to this business of earning a living. It takes more than just rehearsing the speech asking for a raise. We need to make deep reassessments of the importance of work in our lives; struggle backward in memory to the age of ten, before adolescence shipwrecked our ambitions, and remember what we wanted to be when we grew up. Remember what our grown-up selves looked like to us, back when we still thought we had the power to shape our destinies. We need to know that, at least for the time being, while we're alone here, our work is us. Unlike the prince, it can be controlled and used to shape our lives.

The working woman with a family can say, and often does, with pride, "My family always comes first." For us without families, our jobs could come first, but often they don't. Our friends, lovers, even our apartments come first. We may not even like the work we do, and stay only because it's familiar, or because of the pension plan or our friends in the office or simply because it's the job we took while putting our now-ex-husband through medical school.

If work is going to come first, we need to like it, not as a substitute family or a security blanket, but because we like what we *do*. Like it in the same involved, emotional way we were brought up to believe we'd like marriage.

We can change fields. It's easier for us than for others to take night classes and get the necessary degree. We can go band seabirds off the coast of Norway or photograph revolutions or counsel teenage mothers in the inner-city schools or help the Forest Service guard its trees. Mary Ann, a sturdy single friend, is a librarian who suddenly noticed she was spending her weekends complaining about her job, and decided to look for work with a construction company. She has some good contacts to call on, and she likes the idea of building things. I expect she'll do it, and have a marvelous time, and make better money. Who's to stop her?

All we need is courage, and a healthy ingratitude to the place that's been so kindly signing our paychecks.

We have the time and energy, being alone here, to throw ourselves into a heavy commitment to work, and this has spinoff benefits. When the job feels worth spending the day's energy on, the evenings and weekends feel less restless; we need less payback from them, fewer ways to entertain ourselves. We need less input from our friends to reinforce our sense of self; we know who we are. We're the person who's researching the sex lives of echinoderms, or designing the new city park. With that firmly in mind, we can curl up in the evening with a book instead of roaming the city looking for someone to call us by name.

Some of us work from home, through faxes and modems, and according to the seers this is a growing trend, keeping us out of rush-hour traffic and enabling us to spend the whole day in our bathrobes if we choose, going into the actual office only for occasional meetings. Some of us worked at home even before faxes, free-lancing this and that. This is a good idea for people with families, if they can keep the families off the worktable, but those who live alone should look carefully at the isolation. In the office where I sometimes work, various graphic artists have always worked at home and brought the results in to the office. The family men and women among them do what they need to do and rush away again; the single people hang around, sometimes for hours, trying to scratch up conversations.

The human contact at the watercooler is not to be sneezed at. Psychologists hint that those of us who go through our days without faces and voices around can easily go round the bend and start dressing like Napoleon or talking to pigeons. Solitary folk should be wary of such faceless, voiceless freedom. How shall we even end the working day? We turn off the computer and stand up, and we're still where we always were, and still alone.

Conversely, jobs heavy on human contact leave us

content to be alone at home. My once-neighbor Eileen was a physical therapist; all day there were hands snatching at her, reaching out for help, and demands on her sympathy and attention. I asked her if she minded eating alone every night, and she laughed incredulously. She came home to her apartment and her cat, and set the table with a wineglass, an ironed linen napkin, and good silverware. She left the answering machine on and made a salad and an omelet, and poured a glass of wine. She sat down alone, in the cool of solitude, and let her spirit come trickling back to her. She sipped the wine and held out a scrap of omelet to the cat, saying, "Well, little Max, and how was *your* day?"

In the meantime, single folk who worked all day alone, at home or in a laboratory or a lighthouse, were climbing the walls, thirsting for companionship.

Finally, we should consider the satisfactions of the soul, as distinct from those of achievement. Up until recently, it was the recognized job of any women with fewer than five children to shoulder some social burdens not her own, without pay. It was her responsibility to consider the sick and the elderly and the orphan, stray dogs, water polluters, homeless derelicts, threatened wildlife, drunks, women's rights, and abandoned babies. Then these problems were institutionalized, and became state and federal responsibilities, and presently the women went out and got full-time jobs for pay. Now the official responsibility seems to be losing its grip, or retreating in fundless confusion.

Women with both jobs and families don't have the smallest scraps of time or attention to spare for anything more involved than voting; we solitaries do. Some of us already work for virtuous causes in our regular jobs, and awful jobs they often are, depressing and badly paid, but deserving all praise. The rest of us should consider donating some of our energies.

The official word for this is "volunteerism," a word so hideous and unnecessary as to make the stoutest wince, but we can think of it simply as "volunteering." It offers us a dazzling choice of fields, wider than our jobs because it requires no degrees or résumés. We can pick causes close to our hearts; if not politics, then abused animals; if not the cancer ward, then literacy. From where we're sitting, we may feel we don't quite care enough to go out and actually *work*, and perhaps writing a check is enough, but it's the work that fans the spark and makes the thing ours, the way a garden isn't really ours until we've dug and weeded in it. We can't know how much we care till we work, and work long enough to be familiar with the nuts and bolts. Then, if it's still too dull or too heartbreaking we can pick something else.

From the purely selfish point of view, it's good for us.

If we're stuck in disappointing jobs, it supplies the extra satisfaction. If we work in an impersonal field, crunching numbers or burrowing through legal documents, it supplies the human—or animal—touch. It opens out contacts, because friends are more easily made in the common cause of work than at play, where all we have in common is the need for amusement. It keeps us connected, and connection around here is our challenge. And it gives us the essential pat on the soul's back; people with families shovel out virtue and self-sacrifice daily, while those who live alone can go months on end without doing anything totally selfless. A touch of virtue, even of smugness, keeps us in balance.

We might even like our volunteer work better than our regular job; it might even evolve into a regular job. My ex-sister-in-law, for instance, after doing it for free, found herself getting paid to fly around the country finding homes for wild burros and mustangs no longer welcome on their traditional ranges. It's true she also found herself with several burros and mustangs of her own, and you might have to worry about that. You could end up with a houseful of stray dogs or handicapped orphans, or a soup kitchen in your living room, but you might learn to enjoy that too.

Doing is important. We are what we do. Sleepwalking through our work because we feel safe there or sticking to disappointing fields just because we trained for them, we're wasting more than the family woman's working week: she has other purposes, other business, but we're wasting our whole selves.

If we're working mainly for the money, for heaven's sake let's stop blushing and stammering and squeeze every penny out of it. Learn the rules, and play the game bravely and cannily. Make money. Invest it, increase it, use it to make more. Make friends with money in the abstract, as power, instead of as a means to an end.

On the other hand, if money doesn't seem quite the whole point, we can make a quantam leap into a job we'll enjoy the doing of.

Without the support of families at our side, we can be timid about sailing into the unmarked seas, but without family priorities to negotiate around, we're free to sail whenever we get up the nerve.

Chapter 8

Play

Feast often, and use friends not still so
sad,
Whose jests and merriment may make
thee glad.

—EOBANNUS HESSUS

Some of us never go out and some of us never stay home.
The crouchers and the wanderers. The inert and the restless. Recently, in a column of advice on getting my life
together, I read that I should try to stay home two nights
a week. For half of us, two nights at home sounds claustrophobic; for the other half, five nights out on the tiles
sounds even worse.

In the cities, hordes of the unattached, gay and

straight, migrate from bar to bar. They travel singly or in pairs or groups, come in, look around. See who's there. Stay a while and move on. It's always too early to go home, too soon to call it a night, not yet late enough to turn the key in the lock and face the dark silence.

Stores stay open late for us. A New York woman I know spends her evenings compulsively trying on shoes, hour after hour, rather than go home to the unblinking answering machine and the junk mail.

Meanwhile, back in the apartment, the rest of us sit and fiddle with the remote control. Leaf through a magazine and look at our watches: 8:30:29; 8:41:46. In the long days of summer, people are still pouring through the streets; in some areas children are still out playing, and we can't very well go to bed when the bright air is ringing with nine-year-olds crying "Not-it!" We could go out, yes, but it's a lot of trouble to go out. More trouble than staying home.

Families are time-consuming. They make extra work, and they're around a lot; just being with them fills in hours of time. Alone, we have time left over that needs to be filled somehow.

We watch television. Many, maybe most, of us walk into our houses and apartments and flick the thing on as we pass, and go about our business with it yammering away softly, punctuated by bursts of canned laughter, like a houseful of company. Sometimes we hardly notice it; sometimes we sit down and watch it.

Actually watching it is called "viewing" by the people who sell it to us, a word they cooked up as sounding more actively involved than just watching, which sounds pretty passive, and is. We spend, on a national average, twenty-nine hours a week watching the stuff; no doubt those who live alone spend more than the average, having fewer distractions. Once upon a time we apologized and even lied about it. Insisted we watched only "good" programs, documentaries about wars or polar bears; the World Series; four-star movies; news analysis. Now we seem to have thrown snobbery to the winds and hunkered down to watch pretty much anything, and rehash it the next morning around the watercooler. It gives us something in common, a binding thread of shared experience, like weather for gatherings of farmers.

Now we have the VCR too. It was a sociable device in the beginning, as television was in its own early days, and people who owned one invited friends over to watch. If they were good friends, they plugged in the movie and raised their voices slightly and chatted all the way through, glancing at the screen occasionally and asking, "Who are those people? Why are they in Paris?" Now that we each have our own, we watch alone. Even the last snobs have VCRs, telling themselves that a movie with subtitles is an enriching cultural experience not even remotely related to television.

For those who still felt underentertained, cable television came to fill in the blanks. With cable, we can have our watching custom-tailored; movie buffs, sports and rock music fans, news addicts, and even weather addicts need never know an empty moment.

For the married couple, the box is probably a boon and keeps them from killing each other. Pointless quarrels have to be dropped or at least suspended when the program comes on; a rented movie gives them something to talk about before bedtime; a husband on the verge of abandoning his loved ones can defuse himself watching the football game.

For solitaries, though, television is isolating. It's bad for us simply because it keeps us from doing other things, real things, with live action and a cast of real people. Too much canned entertainment can cripple our normal social impulses.

Two of us were invited over one afternoon to visit a third. We chatted for a few minutes, and then our hostess said there was a program she wanted to watch, and did we mind? We were mildly shocked, but there seemed no point in objecting, since she'd already turned on the set. The three of us sat on her couch and watched her television. I forget what the program was; probably something from PBS, since it's so educational you can watch it all day without feeling you're wasting your life. It was pretty slow, and after a while I sneaked a magazine from the rack and turned the pages, wondering what Miss Manners would say and whether it's rude to read during your hostess's television program. When whatever-it-was ended and something else came on, I looked up. "What's this one?" I asked politely.

My hostess glanced at me in confusion, as if wondering what I was doing on her couch, and said, "Oh, just a third-rate British comedy series. I only watch it because there's something I like that comes on afterwards."

My fellow guest and I finished our drinks and presently tiptoed away, letting ourselves out. I think our hostess said good-bye, though maybe she didn't notice.

This is an extreme case, I admit, but a lot of us have slipped into addiction to some degree. It's easy. Rooms with no people in them are not only silent, they don't move. Nothing moves. Turn on the set and pictures talk at you and move around. In some ways they're preferable to real company; they never ask for food or drink, don't smoke, or lapse into gloomy silence, or need to be entertained. They don't go away and leave you, either. The perfect friends. You needn't even put on your coat and boots to go and visit them; they're always right there waiting, ready when you are. If you feel you really must get out for a few minutes, you can make a trip to the video store and come home with Harrison Ford.

We get, if not truly addicted, habituated. Turn off the pictures and we don't know what to do with ourselves. Our eyes and ears feel bored and fretful. Click the button back on and watch the city council debating a new tax, which is so excruciatingly dull we can't possibly accuse ourselves of frivolity. Besides, television brings us messages from the outside world, a kind of talking junk mail, to remind us we're not alone on the planet.

As addiction escalates we start watching movies we've seen before, sitcoms with window-rattling laugh tracks, reruns of game shows, interviews with celebrities. In the final stages we may even start taking an interest in celebrities as if they were actual people.

A grisly prospect, you say, but hardly threatening to people like you, with busy active lives. People like you who only turn it on now and then; who can take it or leave it alone.

You can like hell.

I'm not complaining about the quality of the stuff; I don't think the quality matters. It's the quantity. The amount of time we're offstage, time when we can hardly be said to exist at all in any real sense of the word.

Characters in books and plays never sit down to watch television. People in movies don't watch it. People on television never, ever watch television. Nobody wants to look at or read about people watching a lighted box because they aren't doing anything to look at or read about. They aren't even having something happen to them. Sitting there, they aren't falling in love or taking over a business empire, losing the farm at blackjack, slipping on a banana peel, crashing in the Andes, or getting eaten by big white sharks. They aren't even having interior monologues, planning murders, remembering their true loves, or regretting their misspent youth. They're just there, indistinguishable from the couch.

Watching television, we are not the hero. We aren't even a minor character, the hero's aunt, or a meter maid in the background. We simply aren't in it at all; we're the audience, and an invisible, inaudible audience at that, dragged along behind someone else's story. Turn it off and we reappear, ourselves, for weal or woe.

Even with our cheek on the kitchen table and the vodka bottle rolling across the floor, we're part of our own tragedy, our own lives. Pounding the walls and howling with grief and loneliness, we're working out our own destiny, smack in the center of the stage. In front of the television we're functioning at the lowest possible level of existence, receptacles for other people's sound and movement, unable to join them or answer them, as if we were bound and gagged.

Respondents to a survey I read about voted over-whelmingly that television was their second-greatest plea-sure in life. The first-greatest, they said, was "doing things with their families," which may or may not have included sex; the wording wasn't clear. (It may also have included watching television with their families.) I suppose it follows, then, that for those without families television is life's greatest pleasure.

Solitaire must have been a frightful bore, a game with-out competition or triumphs, but at least people playing solitaire knew they were just killing the hours till bedtime. No one ever counted it a joy in life.

When we aren't working or eating or sleeping, we ought to be playing. Watching a box is a lousy way to play.

So is wandering through the shops trying on shoes, or wandering from bar to bar like mythic characters under a primeval curse, but at least the wanderers are out there moving around, being themselves. The faces they see, however unattractive or hostile, are real faces.

For those of us in sad straits, recovering from grief or rage, television helps us avoid the insides of our heads. It roots out the silence from the remotest hiding places, pokes the demons out from under the bed, and replaces our interior voices with its own voice. The interior voices wait to pounce like patient tigers. Turn the television off in order to go to bed, and after the hours of clatter the silence comes in on padded feet, through the locked windows and barred doors, and squats in all the corners, watching you while you try to sleep. The tiger inches forward.

It's more comfortable, in the long run, to be on terms with the tiger. He won't go away, but if you've been looking into his eyes, at least he can't catch you off guard.

Sweat it out. Pace back and forth in the apartment, relearning such long-neglected talents as crying and biting your fingernails. Wrestle the demons hand-to-hand, like Jacob with the angel. After you've spent the evening with them, it's less of a shock to find them waiting for you in bed.

Those who aren't in the grip of grief, merely bored and idle, should consider substitute fun—a word that has suffered some strange degradation lately, as automation took it over. A few years back when there were video arcades, before every home became a video arcade, I used to pass one on my regular route around town. On its wall, in letters four feet high, it proclaimed: FUN OF YOUR CHOICE! "Fun" is no longer something we have with people; it plugs into the wall socket and operates with buttons and switches.

Once upon a time, apparently, fun was a more natural outgrowth of the human spirit. In the 1660s, after gloomy

Cromwell left the land and England cheered up again, Samuel Pepys kept a diary of his days. He was known as a serious, hardworking man, but in almost every entry a bit of fun creeps in; he slips out of the office to go to the theater; he dances; he bursts into song. Listen to him:

"And after dinner to cards; and about five o'clock, by water to Greenwich; and up to the top of the hill, and there played upon the ground at cards . . ."

"And took the Jemmy yacht down to Woolwich, it being a fine day and a brave gale of wind, and had some oysters brought to us aboard . . ."

"To Deptford, and walked home, and there came into my company three drunken seamen, but one especially, who told me such stories, calling me captain, as made me mighty merry, and they would leap and skip, and kiss what maids they met all the way . . ."

"Over the water to the Jamaica House, and there the girls did run for wagers over the bowling green . . ."

"The play done, I took Mercer by water to Spring Garden, and there with great pleasure walked and ate and drank and sang, making people come about us to hear us, and two little children did come into the arbor, and we made them dance prettily . . ."

"And I to bed, leaving them to their sport and blind man's buff . . ."

"By and by to my house, to a very good supper, and

mighty merry, and good music playing; and after supper to dancing and singing until about twelve at night; and then we had a good sack posset for them, and an excellent cake, and so to dancing again, and singing . . ."

"About eleven, it being very fine moonshine, my wife and Mercer came into the garden and, my business being done, we sang till about twelve at night, with mighty pleasure to ourselves and neighbours, by their casements opening . . ."

"We fell to dancing . . ."

A lot of spontaneous play seems to have leaked out of the world; not even children dance and sing now, and don't tell me we just live in grimmer times. Try bubonic plague for grimness. When we get together with our friends we tend, if we're female, to have long, serious, therapeutic conversations, and if we're male we play racquetball or golf or volleyball, unsmiling. Maybe we ought to gather more often for purposes of merriment, because merriment, unlike eating, sleeping, working, and television, really does require other people, and it's good for us.

Marsilius Ficinus, a sage of old, said, "Live merrily, O my friends, free from cares, perplexity, anguish, grief of mind, live merrily, heaven made you for mirth; again and again I request you to be merry; if anything trouble your hearts, or vex your souls, neglect and contemn it, let it pass. And this I enjoin you, not as a Divine alone, but as a Physician, for without this mirth, which is the life and quintessence of Physick, medicine, and whatsoever is used and applied to prolong the life of man, is dull, dead, and of no force. With Seneca I say, be merry while the fates allow."

We ought to give parties more often; we ought to let ourselves and our friends throw instant parties, without having to clean the whole apartment and call a caterer; parties with jug wine and frozen pizza; sudden gatherings such as our mothers and grandmothers had when they were young and every civilized house had a piano and someone in every group could play it and everyone, whether they could sing or not, sang. We ought to roll up the rugs and dance.

Maybe we should get together and start a political movement to revise fun. Call it the Party Party.

In the meantime, here we are alone with these evenings and these weekends to fill as happily as possible, because it may be a kind of duty to be happy. Those of us who go out seven nights a week because we're afraid of being home alone—What would I do with myself after I've washed my hair? After the rented movie rolls its credits? After the silence comes back?—should reshape our evenings for more play and less aimlessness. Those of us who have fallen lazily or timidly into the habit of staying home should go out. Too many nights alone at home make going out seem vaguely sinister. Threatening. We're safe, or relatively safe, in our familiar apartments and offices, but what dragons crouch behind our walls?

If we're newly alone, we can feel exposed and self-conscious out there in the world, naked on all sides to the winds of the world and the eyes of strangers. This anxiety doesn't apply to going to work or running errands, because it's always acceptable to be busy alone. Being alone and at leisure is embarrassing, especially for women; women are held to be responsible for relationships, so to appear in the world without one is to have failed. We feel shunned, as among the Amish when everyone stops speaking to the transgressor, or expelled, as in biblical times when the criminal was sent out into the desert to die of hunger and loneliness.

We can go anywhere we want to go, but how do we know where we want to go? Our plans have no friction, no resonance, no echo. We say to ourselves, There's a movie at the Ritz I'd like to see, and no one answers. The idea gets no response, pro or con; it hangs in the air and begins to seem thin and pointless. We could call Marianne and see if she'd like to go with us. Or we could just turn on the television instead.

We stay home alone. We call a friend but the friend is out, and we feel rejected by the answering machine. We brood. Why are we locked in here by ourselves? Were we naughty, have we been sent to our room in disgrace while the others are outside playing? Exciting things are waiting to be seen and done, but how can we go see and do them alone?

At certain times of year staying home feels right. When it's spitting sleet and freezing rain outside, and dark before we get home from work, home is the correct place to be. We are not outcasts from the world; we're sheltering cozily in our caves and it's right and proper to do so, the only sensible thing. Make something hot to drink and change into dry slippers and curl up with a stack of magazines, listening to the sleet against the panes. But in spring when we come home from work the sun is still shining. The mail is disappointing. (Mail is always disappointing for the solitary. There's a long chatty letter from a friend, if we're lucky, and a postcard from San Juan, maybe even a check, but we go on riffling hopefully through the catalogs and bills, searching for the message that isn't there, ever.) We look out the window. Across the street a young man rings a doorbell, and presently a pretty girl comes out and the two of them dance away, laughing soundlessly, and there we still are at the window, inside.

October in the temperate zone is bad too. There's a slippery, unsafe feeling in the air, maybe some deep ancient nervousness about the winter, with its hostile weather that feels like the world's hostility. Wind, and the new slant of light in the streets, and a sense of sliding sideways off the face of the earth. Weightlessness. Restlessness. We should go out, go somewhere, even if there's nobody to go with us.

Too long inside our walls and a terrible shyness grips us. Needing company, we shrink from it, stop calling friends or even answering their calls on the tape, and slip into a settled moroseness. Then when we finally do go out our social hinges are rusty. Someone waves to us on the street and our overload lights go on, we gabble maniacally and clutch at their clothing, or fall in love with them. Modern American life makes no provision for ordinary daily human contact outside the workplace; no butchers, milkmen, servants, aunts, farmhands, or delivery boys to see without effort in the course of a Saturday. In order to make contact we need to make plans for it. We have to get up and go out and find it, forge it deliberately in the very teeth of rejection, exposing our solitude in order to cure it, like poor old Uncle Pee-Pee in a raincoat.

For a woman, it's pleasant to have a man to go places with. He needn't be the love of our life, and he needn't replace our women friends, but going out with a man feels traditional, and the world approves. A man and a woman sitting on a park bench, buying hot dogs at the baseball game, waiting in the ski-lift line, standing in the lobby arguing about the first act or the first violinist, reading the menu; they form an acceptable, suitable unit.

If we've been used to appearing in public with a man, another woman can feel like second choice. Not at lunch time, of course, when women have traditionally congregated, but in the evening. We feel we've lost some status; we look like rejects. We think we're being inspected with pity and contempt: See the poor twittering hens, no man wanted to take them out, they've been forced back on each other's company, they won't be able to figure the tip.

Perhaps we won't. As if in mute, mulish protest against manlessness, a surprising number of otherwise competent women go brain-dead at the sight of a restaurant check. Women who can figure their own taxes without shedding a tear break down completely when asked to find 15 percent of $32.80 and divide it by two. Maybe tips act as a magnet for all our insecurities. Maybe they're the final exam on our ability to survive on our own; will we leave too much, out of nervous apology for our lives, or not enough, out of sheer incompetence? Change is dug for, laid down, picked up again, dollars passed back and forth, and we say, "No, you put down too much, didn't you? Let me see the check again. All right, two times three is six . . ."

To find 10 percent of the bill, mentally move the decimal point one place to the left: $32.80 gives you roughly $3.30. Twice that, or $6.60, is 20 percent. Adjust the tip somewhere between the two, depending on the place and the service, and divide it between you. Surely we can manage this in our heads without looking like fools and incurring the contempt of surrounding tables.

We can go out to dinner with someone. Or we can join a Great Books Discussion group, a therapeutic support group, or a bridge club. We can go to the nearest shopping mall and walk around and around looking at merchandise. We can work; lots of us do. Many or even most of the solitary people I know work late in the evenings. Maybe some of what they're doing is essential and really needs to be done in the evenings; maybe not. They come home at nine or ten, turn on the television, nuke a frozen dinner, and go to bed, relieved for another day of the need to fill in time. According to a Harris survey, American leisure time has shriveled by 32 percent since 1973. That means us, probably, hanging around in our offices, getting to know the cleaning women, postponing the key in the lock at home.

We can hang out in bars, hoping to meet someone, or hang out in bars hoping for nothing. (Middle-aged women, lonely to the point of madness, sit at the bar in the dusty afternoon light from the window, drinking Manhattans and muttering. Middle-aged men in hats try to strike up a conversation with the bartender; they pick lunatic quarrels with strangers.)

We can sign up for courses. This is fine if we actually go to them. Many of us, spring and fall, sign up for a class in yoga or calligraphy or square dancing or Eastern religions or flower-drying, and go once, and then the next time it's too much trouble, or it's dark out, or we've already taken our shoes off and we might be coming down with a cold. Classes work out better if we're doing them for a reason other than getting out of the house; a degree or a specific job. Otherwise they feel like busywork, and unless we find merry and sociable company in them we can quickly wear out our interest in flower-drying.

Some of us are more easily entertained than others. My dentist's new hygienist, a widow with grown children, had just moved to the city from a small town, and she was having the time of her life. "There's so much to do!" she chirruped. When she let me rinse and spit, I asked her what she'd done lately, what metropolitan delights she'd found.

"I went to the dog show last weekend," she said.

"I'd never been to a dog show before. It was fascinating. There were so many dogs! There was a Portuguese water spaniel, I'd never even heard of those before, have you? There were lots of dogs I'd never heard of before. So many different kinds! I really love living in the city."

I asked, after the next rinse, if she had a dog herself.

"I did have one once," she said, "years ago, but of course I couldn't have one in the apartment. The show was fascinating though. The obedience trials were so funny." She chuckled. "One dog wouldn't do *anything* he was supposed to do."

I felt rebuked in my idleness, surrounded by such entertainments, and when I got home I opened the newspaper to check the abundance the city offered for my evenings and weekends.

A housewarming at the Women's Alliance and a crafts festival at a church and a potluck supper at the Men's Collective.

A costume party at a nightclub.

A Gay Pride celebration, a rollerskating marathon, and a free cholesterol screening.

A flower show called "Pollination" and a Hadassah trip to a spa.

The Gay Community Center had a knitting workshop and the Garden Club had a bazaar.

A branch library was having a juggling exhibit, but it was far away in the boondocks.

There were several flea markets, a used-book sale, and a trip to the seashore for Senior Citizens.

Speeches were to be given on the Architecture of Washington, the Common Market, and Dolls for Democracy.

The Optimist Club had a meeting, the Crisis Intervention Network a banquet, and the Citizens Committee a symposium on education.

Someone was giving a lecture on how to break into soap operas.

I had a choice of sixteen workshops: working mothers, games for children, massage for health, acting, longevity, secretaries, sign language, photography, emotions, meditation, smoking, sexual awareness (but I'm trying to cut *down* on that), reproductive rights, the Age of Thirty, magazine writing, and tapping into the memories of my previous lives.

There were classes in jazz, a slide lecture on Russia, and a meeting of Jewish feminists.

A festival of contemporary music. Three plays, twenty-one movies, and five dance workshops.

I considered Dolls for Democracy, the most inscrutable offering, but it was only a speech, and listening to speeches is low on the merriment scale. Instead I went to the Garden Club bazaar, which was tiny and silent, in a brick courtyard. The woman at the sales table was reading a paperback. Alone, I walked around the displays for five minutes and then bought a box of petunia seedlings to take home to die on my windowsill.

The next day I went to one of the art galleries, which was even quieter. The only other person there was a furious-looking little man, almost certainly the artist, who glared at me so pointedly that I spent longer than I'd intended smiling blindly at his paintings.

In another part of the paper I saw that the university was offering a non-credit course called "How to Have Fun." I thought for a while about this, and all the students wearing paper party hats and taking notes, but I didn't go.

Maybe nobody did. Maybe everyone stayed home with a videotape of *Casablanca*.

Wistfully I considered Mr. Pepys, fellow of the Royal Society and pillar of the British Navy Office, singing in his back yard and playing cards on a hilltop. Aside from electronics, most of our leisure seems to involve either watching other people do things or improving ourselves by learning to be more—or less—something-or-other. Actually doing things, aside from all that diligent exercising the right people have taken up, is hard to come by.

If we have exciting work of our own that we can do alone, after hours, then that's a help and a privilege, especially in times of crisis. A painter I know found himself alone in the world for the first time, at the age of twenty-eight, and it threw him into such a panic that all he could do was work. He finished a dozen large canvases in less than a month, painting and painting, the radio blaring away at his elbow, ten, twelve, fourteen hours a day. If he put down his brushes or turned off the radio he burst into tears, so he had to keep painting. It was wonderful work, too, obsessive and brilliant, his best. After he found a nice girl and moved in with her it was never the same again.

This isn't for everyone, alas; if *I* filled in the long evenings covering canvas with paint, it would be considered vandalism rather than work. It helps if we can feel we've accomplished something constructive.

We can ferret out and connect with clubs and groups that go forth and do interesting things: bird-watching, skiing, hiking, camping, wildflower-watching. A lot of this is good exercise, and better qualified as fun than jogging or weight lifting. I belonged, for a while, to a club that investigated a variety of the sort of thing you wouldn't go off and do on your own. We went rock-climbing, soar-planing, ballooning, kayaking, skiing, and, one wild day, scrambling on muleback for seven hours through semi-permeable woods and streams in the Pocono Mountains. The club's leader, who lived alone, had formed the group so he wouldn't have to sit around by himself on weekends. It worked almost too well, what with everyone calling him day and night to ask if they'd get their money back if it rained, and whether to bring a sweater, and did they get a discount for bringing their own tent.

Doing something is better than doing nothing, but doing nothing may be better than cleaning the apartment all weekend. I know quite a few women and even some men who consider housework an acceptable use of leisure. It isn't. With only ourselves to befoul our quarters, they probably aren't dirty anyway, and if they are, perhaps we like them that way; perhaps we feel safer and cozier in a nest of rumpled clothing and magazines. Life is too short to dust things that don't have dust on them, and tidiness, like fitness, can mushroom into an unwholesome obsession for the solitary. When we have no more clean underwear or saucepans we can gather them up and deal with them, and make a few paths through our rooms so we don't step on our earrings or slip on the newspapers. Otherwise, if it doesn't smell bad, breed, or block the bathroom door, don't hassle it. These are our own quarters, and we get no Brownie points for cleanliness here. We could almost consider housework self-indulgent, since no one benefits but us. We need company, stimulation, refreshment, faces and voices, play. Housework is none of the above.

The exception to this is the refrigerator. We should

look inside it regularly, and throw out the rest of the celery, because it's hard enough to feed ourselves decently when we *aren't* afraid to open that door. (Do not feel guilty. It is not our fault that celery grows only in bunches large enough to feed Yugoslavia. Three quarters of all celery grown worldwide gets thrown away sooner or later, and sooner is less repulsive than later.)

Exercise for exercise's sake is not, as mentioned earlier, play, but there's nothing wrong with incidental exercise incurred while square dancing, surfing, or chipping rocks looking for fossil ferns.

Which brings us to consider the serious hobby. "Hobby" has taken on a silly, futile, time-wasting connotation, and we think immediately of macrame owls, crooked birdhouses assembled from a kit, collections of beer cans, paint-by-number landscapes, decorated place mats, and the arts and crafts suitable for the insane, the senile, and small children on rainy days at summer camp. All real, worthwhile work is now supposed to be done by trained professionals, and the word "amateur" now means clumsy and inept instead of one who works for the love of it. The vigorous intellectual curiosity that drove our ancestors to investigate seems to have narrowed. We learn what we need to learn to earn our livings, and leave the whole vast rest of life to people who earn their livings in those other fields. Even music, once something everyone made, is now strictly for professionals, and produced by expensive audio equipment instead of by our own hands and voices.

In the seventeenth, eighteenth, and nineteenth centuries, it was taken for granted that intelligent people would have serious interests beyond earning a living, and study some of them seriously enough to make real contributions. Even women, if they were single or had plenty of servants, joined in. Uneducated maiden ladies did more than write novels and verse; they explored uncharted deserts and made their marks on ornithology or botany or geography without any credentials at all. Professionals listened to amateurs, unthinkable today. Bank clerks were respected paleontologists on weekends, butchers could be geologists, and after-hours astronomers made important discoveries by sitting on hilltops keeping notes on the sky until the sun came up and it was time to go to work.

These days, just being allowed to learn is professionalized and expensive. If we want to learn, we're supposed to enroll in a course at a recognized university and be informed by an accredited authority. The old-time freelance curiosity is discouraged; no more may we just read and watch, ask questions, correspond with the experts, keep field notes and make sketches, and hang around where the work is done, figuring it out for ourselves. We are still allowed in libraries, though. Probably that expensive, accredited professor has written some books we're allowed to read.

It would be good for us all if we could lift amateur hobbying out of its current disreputable swamp of commercially sponsored knickknacks into respectability again. All we need, really, is to take our extracurricular pastimes more seriously. Here we are with all this time we aren't spending picking up the kids from band practice or dropping our husband's pants off at the cleaners; we deserve something more from our hours than the electronic fun of our choice. If we like wildflowers, we can learn botanical drawing. If we carry a camera, we can study its technicalities, buy a tripod and a light meter. As long as we love what we do, it's play, and qualifies as the refreshment we need. And if we take it seriously enough for long enough, we could end up getting paid for it, and find ourselves with work that's really play, life's highest blessing. Certainly our Sunday afternoons will move faster. Probably we'll find like-minded people to play with, people for field trips and advice, for conversations more absorbing than the flaws of former lovers. We'll find something to do on vacations.

If we're newly alone because of death or divorce, or because the person we lived with stuck a note on the refrigerator and moved to San Francisco, vacations can gape before us like the edge of the world. Where are we allowed to go, all by ourselves, and what will happen to us alone? How can we walk into the unknown and leave the friendly murmur of the office and its structured days, our familiar furniture that recognizes our footsteps?

While we're still feeling anxious and bruised, it's a good idea to holiday in a friendly burrow. If we have kind, clucking parents we can go for a visit, a duty expected of the single in any case, and walk their dog, smile at their neighbors, watch television in the evenings, dodge the well-meaning questions and eat what's put in front of us. Comforted, we'll soon be bored enough to look forward to home and solitude.

If we don't have hospitable parents, a friend's couch will serve, preferably in a different sort of setting. Many of us make a point of cultivating friends in interesting places. Visiting around is one of the glories of being unattached. We learn to be good guests, make charming conversation, and play with the kids. Unwelcome as we may be at dinner parties, we're a lot less trouble visiting, sleeping solo on the couch, than if we were trailing a husband and a passel of children.

By the next vacation we'll feel stronger, though maybe never totally independent, vacation-wise. In a perfect world, each of us would have a charming member of the opposite sex with whom to go traveling, and indeed it's one of the most frequent appeals in the Personals ads, but life has its flaws and we may have to make other arrangements. Even our dearest friends may have commitments in different directions. We may have to go alone.

My friend Bruce, finding himself at thirty-five unemployed and unattached, set off to see the world. In the past year he has been to Rio, Paris, London, Buenos Aires, Bangkok, Tokyo, Hong Kong, Nepal, Delhi, Calcutta, and Tibet. He has explored Easter Island on horseback, and looked over the edge at the end of things in Tierra del Fuego. Traveling cheap, he eats in street-corner cafés and sleeps in bed-and-breakfasts. Meeting fellow travelers, he collects invitations to visit them, and in the future he'll be welcome on couches all over the world. My refrigerator door flowers exotically with postcards. Bruce the Frequent Flyer—an example to us all.

It's too bad that travelin' down that lonesome road is a metaphor for going through life with nobody to hold our hand, because the real roads we take alone can offer up more of their secrets than roads taken in company. Alone, we're more likely to meet and talk to strangers along the way, and we notice more. However, there's no denying that solitary travel has its drawbacks; no one will stand by the luggage while we go to the bathroom, so we have to drag it into the stall with us. Asking for a single room, we give hoteliers apoplexy, and we'll pay so much extra we might as well be twins. Single rooms, where they're available at all, tend to be dark and shabby and closet-sized, overlooking an airshaft. The restaurant owner isn't pleased to see us either, or that unprofitable empty chair at our table for two.

In some areas it's downright dangerous to be solitary and female, and in some it just feels that way. No matter how modestly we dress and speak and how carefully we choose our hotels and transportation, in some countries a lone American woman is going to be hassled. There will always be places, risks, adventures, possibilities we will never chance on our own. In the past, solitary women have done some notable adventuring, but most of us probably won't set out for Borneo or Tibet or the South Pole without company. No matter. There are other places, and company available too.

Group vacations have come a long way, and no longer feel slightly shameful, as if we hadn't the gumption to strike out on our own. The everything-included resort like Club Med is still a slightly static option, taking much of the stress and all of the adventure out of visiting foreign lands; how much fun we have there depends too heavily on whom we meet. It's a mistake to set forth hoping to meet someone marvelous, because of the possibility of disappointment: if we go to see Paris we will surely see Paris; if we go to find love we may not.

The best group journeys have a purpose, giving their

members something in common to talk about. These come in an astonishing variety of flavors, and we can choose to go in search of gardens, mountains, whales, Roman ruins, art, wine, history, sailboats, water birds, or total mastery of French. We can turn to our dinner partner and say, "I don't understand the depth-of-field preview on my camera," and make more social progress than at a singles gathering where the company has assembled for the sole purpose of sizing each other up. We will almost certainly find pleasant company among the like-minded travelers, even if we never see our new friends again. Married couples, far from the orderly gavotte of their married social lives, are more accessible for friendship, and the unmarried more ready to open their hearts at a cooking class in Tuscany than at home.

Besides, there's someone in charge. Traveling alone, having left our familiar walls and houseplants and dentist behind, we feel more vulnerable and need a hand to hold, a group leader to deal with lost luggage and tell us how many guilders to the dollar.

At worst, the group will be composed of equal parts of bores and whiners, all wearing embarrassing clothes and making loud embarrassing comments, shepherded by a desperate but chirpy leader spouting enthusiastic set speeches on the charms of the Pyramids, the Cotswolds, the Hermitage, the peasantry, and the boiled cabbage.

At best, we will learn something, meet entertaining people, and have a safe adventure.

Medium-sized groups are best. If there are only seven other people, we may hate them all and, alone, have no one to talk to. With more than thirty, progress is so cumbersome the tour seems encased in cement. Every large tour has one person who's pathologically late, and even though the leader says several times that the bus will wait for no one, it always waits. Forever, if need be. Only the largest, most commercial hotels and restaurants will take you in. Small villages, churches, ports, and gardens are overwhelmed by you; you replace the native population. Large tours are planned around the average traveler's desires, and you begin to feel like a sheep, or a lemming, pursuing the average dream.

When it works out, traveling with a dear friend is probably best of all. (Of course if you happen to be madly in love with each other, you really might as well save the airfare and stay home in bed, since you'll barely notice the Pyramids.) Unfortunately it's hard to judge a friend's traveling style until you try. The chronic griper can be entertaining at lunch but infuriating in Mexico. One of you may travel with a change of socks and a toothbrush while the other has four stone suitcases and a cooler full of spare food. One wants to mingle with the natives and eavesdrop in the bazaar while the other feels safest in the hotel room watching English-language television. One needs a rest while the other feels that every moment spent stationary is a moment thrown in the trash. It's always worth trying, though, because the rewards are ample and, with someone by our side, the unforeseen looks less life-threatening and more like an adventure.

With the vacation spent and over, we still have all those weekends. They're easy to fritter away—errands and laundry on Saturday, the crossword puzzle on Sunday, maybe brunch and a movie—but a change of scenery re-charges us better. Get in a car and drive somewhere, with or without a friend.

We're a nation of car drivers, and being in "the driver's seat" means being in charge of our lives. The lone woman who likes fast cars and drives them boldly down life's highways is one of our healthier specimens. To creep apologetically along in the slow lane with both hands on the wheel, testing it for the wobble that means the wheels are about to fall off, is a sign that we're losing our grip. Anxiety is creeping up our tailpipe.

That's why we have radios in cars. Driving alone at night, when it seems years since we've seen a light and possibly we're on the wrong road anyway, going the wrong direction, the engine starts making those ominous sounds it so rarely makes by daylight, on familiar streets. The metaphor stalks us: we are alone in the dark on a strange road, heading for the unknown. We turn the radio up louder and sing along with the golden oldies, still straining to hear, through the racket, the sound of approaching engine failure.

Then, too, those of us who once lived with a man may have trusted him to cope with the car; perhaps cars really need a man around, we feel, to keep them in line. Perhaps cars maintained only by women are less reliable. Alone, maybe we've neglected some simple routine, failed to tighten the bolt that holds the whole thing together.

Gone are the days when businesslike freckled teenagers advised and helped us whenever we stopped for gas. Now the least ept of us is expected to wield a knowledgeable dipstick and carry a tire-pressure gauge in her pocketbook. In all but the most populous areas, we pump our own gas and go on our way with the fumes rising up from our shoes. We're lucky if we can even find a human creature in the station to tell us which way is north. We're on our own. Some day we'll have to change a tire.

When anxiety rises, opt for the business route and the friendly traffic light still blinking red in the sleeping town. Check into a motel; drive by daylight.

Keep a weather eye out for the truck squeeze, a game reported by many solitary women drivers, in which several eighteen-wheelers, hunting in a pack, can force you into the far left lane and keep you there, upping the ante to eighty miles an hour as you go rocketing down the hill toward the curve at the bottom and the bridge where the road narrows. I'm sure most truckers are perfect gentlemen, but there are those who consider cars, especially little ones driven by women, as a species of four-wheeled cockroach.

All travel, adventure, movement, is worth considerable risk and cash. We need to vary our lives. Life in a family changes hourly, like the weather in April, but life alone can sink into a numbing sameness, punctuated only by whether or not the cat has thrown up on the rug today. We need to keep stirring our days so they don't congeal.

We need to invent new fun. Less-competitive fun. Games, in our striving, ambitious society, have lost some of their merriment; somebody wins, the rest lose. We invite our friends over, not for sack posset and singing, like Pepys, but to beat the hell out of them at Scrabble, which leaves a darkness in the air later. Bridge partners stalk out of the house quarreling, and I've seen intelligent adults sulk for hours after going bust at Monopoly. Seldom have I heard such bitterness as from a woman complaining of her morning tennis partner. We care who wins, which is wholesome and leads to financial success in life, no doubt, but hampers the joy of playing. Doesn't anyone still own a Frisbee? Or did Frisbee too develop rules, with winners and losers?

For sanity's sake, let us go forth and see new sights; let us play with our friends for pleasure, and hold the long yellow dogs of melancholy at bay.

Chapter 9

Depression

It is a melancholy of mine own,
compounded of many simples,
extracted from many objects . . .

—SHAKESPEARE

The state of gloom, boredom, inaction, and nonspecific sadness is now officially called depression. This sounds dignified and psychoanalytic, and becomes an acceptable excuse, like a broken leg, for not doing things we ought to do. Unlike grief, it's a recognized malady treated by drugs and supportive therapy. Three hundred years ago it was called "melancholy," and treated by different drugs and different therapy.

Sometimes there's a direct reason for it, making it less dignified and possibly less treatable, and sometimes there's no reason, or no visible one. It comes in various sizes—short, medium, and long—and after you've survived a few bouts you realize they aren't permanent, and if you don't shoot yourself they usually go away. The people in charge of naming our troubles have recently come up with "RBO," or Recurring Brief Depression, affecting, they say, twice as many women as men and lasting for about three days, perhaps to return in two or three weeks. (This is not to be confused with SAD, or Seasonal Affective Disorder, in which you feel rotten because it gets dark so early in the winter. Some people feel a lot better if they know the correct names for things. Others don't much care.)

Mostly when depressed we ride it out, like a cold, making little hopeful efforts to move it along. We stay alert for triggering agents, like a snub from a stranger, a week of rain, or catching an earring in our turtleneck, so the only escape seems to be to cut off our ear, since we're all alone and there's no one to help unfasten it. Sometimes we can see the depression coming before it sees us, and take steps to ward it off.

Grief is trickier. Instead of lying heavily on our days like a wet rug, it plays cat-and-mouse with us. It hides in the bushes. We find ourselves laughing and chatting, and then we pass a familiar street or catch a whiff of someone's after-shave in the elevator, and it pounces. It's harder to fight because it's harder to get a steady look at it; when we try to catch hold of it our hands bleed. We thrust it out of our daily lives and it creeps back in dreams and we wake in tears.

As time goes by our losses start to add up. We're told that life should be a process of accumulation, the getting of new things to add to the old—new friends, lovers, families, jobs, dishes and silverware, interests and affections. And we try, we do try to keep moving forward, and then one day after we've burned our fingers on the broiler, we remember what we used to have and somehow managed to lose. The room fills up with the absent. The lover who said we had the eyes of a poet is married and lives in Cleveland; the lawn is full of the ghosts of children dancing after lightning bugs. Years after the divorce we wake in the night with the awful conviction that it was a mistake, and nothing can be done about it now. Friends have left town forever and dropped out of our lives.

We're a shifty, sliding population. We keep saying, "I may be transferred to Kansas City"—"I've been accepted at the University of Oregon"—"I have an interview for a job in Boston"—"Have you heard from Betsy?"—"I'd write if I had their new address"—"Does anyone know what happened to Tom?"

We used to ask people where they were from, and

they used to know. Now when we ask they look confused, as if trying to remember, and then say, "You mean, where was I born?" We move, they move, motion is our natural element and loneliness lives in our luggage. What we refer to as "home" may be a place we haven't seen in years; a place where there's no one left who knows our name.

Parents die, or retreat into the vagueness of age and lose interest in us. They only want to talk about Medicare, or arthritis, and we feel alone in a peculiarly chilly way when we first realize that our mother, our own mother, doesn't much care that we lost our job or found our true love; we're less important to her than her breakfast.

We work hard and our work comes to less than we'd expected. No one wants to hear about the shadow that showed up on our X-rays. In summer we sit alone and the sun shines in the streets; it's playtime and we're wasting it. In winter the dark closes down like a metaphor for death.

Reasons enough for grief, God knows, and no way to get rid of them. The particular sharp pain of a given loss will fade in a year or two and take its place among the other losses that can't be offset by gains because life doesn't work that way: the four-year-old within us wants it all, wants to have lost nothing and no one.

Grief comes and goes, flickering like heat lightning. After the decent period of true mourning, we can take small precautions against it, put the photographs away in a box, stop playing the old songs, stop encouraging it. One woman I know makes a daily four-block detour on her way to work in order to walk past her ex-husband's parked car and arrive in the office crying. This is like taking your flu out for a good roll in the snow. We must learn to take care of ourselves; no one else will.

Depression doesn't flicker like grief. It settles down over our days like a bad smell—perhaps a dead rat in the wall—and seeps into everything.

Depression is when you drop something on the floor and for days it's too much trouble to pick it up. When you make yourself start to do something and don't finish; leave the underwear and dishes to soak instead of washing them, and on Tuesday they're still soaking. When you accept an invitation because it's too much work to say no, and then don't go because it's raining. When you lose small things like the can opener from sheer inattention. Don't call back the people who left messages on your tape. Keep wearing the same clothes rather than think of anything else to wear. Start to fry an egg and the yolk breaks, so you decide not to eat anything at all.

The mess in the living room changes character. A good mess is a jumble of shoes and library books and flute music and somebody's scarf and ticket stubs and the tapes we were playing last night and an empty wine bottle and the glasses therefrom. A bad mess is made of unread week-old newspapers, unopened mail, a tunafish can, cold coffee with a film of dust on its surface, the box from a frozen dinner, and the pens and paper clips and nickels we dropped on the floor and never picked up.

For the solitary, certain seasons are so traditionally depressive they're almost obligatory. Like Christmas.

Some of us keep hoping they'll cancel it this year, but somehow they never do. It comes around annually, like IRS forms in the mail, and has to be dealt with, and we should plan ahead not to spend it sitting here listening for the laughter of other people's families.

We can take our vacation over Christmas, spending it in some sunny palm-treed spot where it loses its burden of echoes; if we have enough money we can travel all the way to some non-Christian country where it passes harmlessly over our heads as an ordinary day. Wherever we go, we can hope for a touch of dysentery or seasickness to take our mind off it. We can meet other people similarly bent on escape.

We can visit friends or relatives. Some families prefer to seal themselves off in airless bliss at Christmas, but others really long for visitors to diffuse some of the pressure. We arrive loaded with packages, snowflakes in our hair, ready to help with preparations for the party, only mildly saddened that it isn't our own.

We can go out Christmas shopping and spend every penny on ourselves, having sent inexpensive cards to everyone else. Buy something that adds a little needed entertainment and responsibility to our lives—a puppy, or a parrot with a vicious vocabulary to embarrass our guests.

We can give a party, working ourselves into a nervous frenzy with planning and cleaning and cooking, or locate a charity that gives Christmas dinners for the homeless and work for that.

Once in a while a Christmas comes when none of these things pan out. Traveling companions cancel; host and hostess have come down with a virus; our credit cards have been stretched to the breaking point. We're faced with actually spending Christmas in friendless, familyless solitude. We might as well wallow in an orgy of self-pity at this point; if depression is inevitable, make the most of it. Hell, it *is* sad. We shall deck the halls with old snapshots: a lover, long gone now, standing on a chair to fasten the star on the tree; our own little children, if we had some, back when they were too young to demand brand-name electronics; our ex-husband nailing a wreath on our first front door. O what has happened to us since those days of hope and promise? How have we wandered into this sad street?

We shall hang limp empty stockings for all the people we will never, never see again. Trim a tree, a scrawny little tree already losing its needles, and inhale its sad celebrative smell of Christmas past. Roast a Cornish game hen, miniature turkey of the abandoned. Stand at the window, a ball of wet Kleenex in hand, and watch the loving couples and happy families go caroling by outside.

After a while this gets to be good for a quiet giggle. We may even manage to remember the moldy underside of all this rosy nonsense: toys that wouldn't run or couldn't be assembled or needed batteries nobody bought; ties and earrings never to be worn; the year we dropped the gravy boat; disappointment, indigestion. Boring aunts, bossy sisters, envy, ingratitude, hangovers. The year we thought, irrationally, that we were going to get a pony and had to settle for a book of horse stories instead. The year we gave him that gaudy madras jacket and he gave us three pairs of socks, and we both pretended to be overwhelmed, smiling with hatred in our hearts. The kitchen after the grand family dinner, like a battlefield abandoned by the survivors, and the sudden conviction that our skirt doesn't fit any more and won't for a long, long time. The creak of family ties stretched beyond endurance; children who got up too early quarreling drearily in front of the television; the long slide into emotional exhaustion as the day gets late but not, alas, late enough for our in-laws to get up and go home.

Presently we rise and blow our nose, put on our coat and go out to a movie. Which is more than we could do surrounded by a bunch of loved ones.

Of course, if attacked by the true, or dark purple, depression we won't go to a movie or anywhere else. We can't.

In *Anatomy of Melancholy*, Robert Burton says of the depressed, "Such is their laziness, dullness, they will not compose themselves to do ought; they cannot abide work, though it be necessary, easy, as to dress themselves, write a letter, or the like." He quotes a classical sage as noting that "the melancholy are the most part slothful and taciturn; they will scarce be compelled to do that which concerns them, though it be for their good, so diffident, so dull."

Just when we most need stimulation, we're the least able to find it. When we most need decent nourishment, we sink to snacks and junk and coffee warmed over and over in the microwave; when we most need sleep to knit up the raveled sleeve of care we wake at three and lie there with the nameless ache under the ribs, too tired to read or dress, our eyes wide open.

The disease tends to preclude its cure. We have to keep watching it for a break in the clouds or at least a brightening in the west, so we can seize ourselves firmly and rush out for some entertainment, exercise, company. Floss our teeth. Try to get the spiritual blood moving again.

Depression isn't the exclusive property of those who live alone; people embedded in happy families also come down with it, but they seldom sink so far, being kept in motion by a thousand small necessary errands and conversations, perhaps sometimes even getting the unrequested kiss. Alone, we can go down a long way. Our friends would be happy to cheer us up, only we haven't answered any of their calls lately, or gone to any of their parties.

The disease has been around for a long time and collected a lot of cures. Burton recommends the herbs bugloss and borage steeped in wine; they exhilarate the heart, he says. Also, "Laurentius speaks of baths of milk, which I find approved by many others. And still, after the bath, the body to be anointed with oil of bitter Almonds, of violets, new or fresh butter, Capon's grease, especially of the back bone, and then, lotions of the head, embrocations, &c."

For those of us too besotted with gloom to take an ordinary shower, it seems a lot to ask that we bathe in milk and violets, but certainly the effort involved in getting all that stuff together would be good for us.

Furthermore, "the air in our chambers, according to Guianerus, should be moistened with water, and sweet herbs boiled in it, vine and sallow leaves, &c." Perhaps an ordinary vaporizer, with a handful of vine leaves in it? Or maybe a handful of cloves and cinnamon instead of the Vicks? Perhaps simmered in a kettle on the stove?

"Of colors, it is good to behold green, red, yellow, and white, and by all means to have light enough with windows in the day, wax candles in the night, neat chambers, good fires in winter, merry companions; for though melancholy persons love to be dark and alone, yet darkness is a great increaser of the humor." All very sound advice, but who will come bringing merry companions, neaten our chambers, and build us a fire?

Various herbal remedies have been recommended since classical times, especially rosemary. Here's an old recipe: one tablespoon rosemary, one teaspoon sage, and an ounce of peppermint, dried and mixed together; make a tea by steeping a heaping teaspoonful in a cup of boiling water for a minute. It's an odd and interesting flavor, improved by a dash of honey, and it's said to cheer the heart. Can't hurt it, anyway.

If we can't actually muster the energy to get out and go somewhere, at least we can plan to do so; send for travel folders, call a friend about a trip next weekend, or next summer. Planning opens the possibility that life will not always be this gray, that the scenery will change. Burton says, "No better Physick for a melancholy man than change of air and variety of places, to travel abroad and see fashions." (By "abroad," he means out of the house, not necessarily Provence, though Provence would be nice.)

Variety in general is highly recommended as both preventative and cure. "Celius adviseth him that will continue his health to have diversity of callings, occupations, to be busied about, sometimes to live in the city, sometimes in the country; now to study or work, to be intent, then again to hawk, or hunt, swim, run, ride, or exercise himself."

Keep busy. As Dr. Johnson pontificated, "If solitary, be not idle. If idle, be not solitary." "Whilst they are any ways employed," Burton says, "in action, discourse, about any business, sport, or recreation, or in company to their liking, they are very well; but if alone or idle, tormented instantly again [by] a kind of numbing laziness . . ." Ah, yes. Indeed. The hobbies, the extracurricular interests. Useful as prevention, maybe, but once we're sunk in the limp dim spiritless depths of depression we're hardly in shape to plunge into skiing or needlepoint lessons.

We might just manage joining a support group. At this writing, support groups are about the fastest-growing industry in the country, with an estimated 500,000 of them supporting some fifteen million Americans a week for a variety of problems. Most of them are dedicated to helping us blame someone else, usually our parents, for our troubles. What previous generations called whining is now called therapy, and many claim to benefit from it. Support groups differ from group therapy in that there's no boss, no professionally qualified leader who feels just fine and thinks he knows what ails us better than we do. In a support group no one's in charge; everyone feels equally awful, equally co-dependent or abused or depressed.

Of course there's the consideration that a roomful of deeply depressed people wouldn't be very merry company. Still, it would get you out of the house and you might make some new friends, always a cheering prospect.

If we can afford it and can find the right one, we can try a private therapist. I know people who have been very happy with theirs, and visit them on an ad hoc basis, when the need arises, and consider them in the light of close and sympathetic but sensible friends. Just picking one out of the phone book is probably a waste of time and money; get recommendations from like-minded people.

Soon, or perhaps already, we can simply buy the software. Recent experiments with computerized therapy for depression have been encouraging, and I'm told it could cost as little as fifty cents an hour. The program asks us comforting questions, like "Why are you feeling so rotten?" and offers multiple-choice answers. It even assigns homework, like "Go out and meet people." After a trial period, the patients in the experiment felt just as much better as the control group treated by live therapists, and very much better than the third group, left to stew in its own juice.

It's a humbling thought, that our anguish of soul can be cured by conversation with an electronic device, and our sorrows treated in snappy sessions at the home or office keyboard. The possibilities for expansion are limitless; no doubt future programs will simulate the perfect lover, the perfect parents, the perfect friend.

If our gloom is deepening dangerously and we really can't cope, our doctor has emergency chemical help for us. There's no shame attached to grabbing for it, as long as we understand the possibility of becoming co-dependent on our neighborhood druggist.

If there's an obvious reason for the gloom, like Christmas or three days of rain, we can ride it out, confident of change. If we're in love with someone who hasn't returned our calls for a week, that gets filed under "Life," not "Depression."

Sometimes an accidental happening swoops down and sweeps the fog away. A genuine crisis—a fire, a friend in danger—will do it, or some small event that shifts our focus on ourselves.

I had been plunged in the post-holiday darkness for a month. Four Sundays' worth of newspapers lay unread on the floor. I'd been using the last bath towel for a week, when I bothered to bathe at all, and eating what I found in the kitchen cupboards—noodles, oatmeal, bouillon cubes—too idle to shop.

Then one day I noticed myself trying to whistle while cleaning the cat's pan and stopped to look around. Pounds and pounds of newspapers had been scanned, baled, and recycled; mail had been read and bills paid; a stew was simmering on the stove; friends were expected. I was just back from the Laundromat and everything washable was clean and folded, and there I was scrubbing the cat's pan and whistling.

What had happened? Certainly not spring; outside it was still another black, wet, filthy-looking Sunday in a city apparently abandoned by everyone but me. Just the same, I felt better. I felt fine, in fact, and sat down to consider, and came up with a rather embarrassing clue.

I'd dragged myself out to the country to see a dear old friend. Her lane was too steep to plow, and we'd left her car in the road and were climbing through deep crusty snow to her house. A sedentary type, my friend had borrowed a pair of ski poles for the ascent, and was huffing valiantly in my wake as I strode ahead to break trail. Every five or six steps we stopped so she could rest.

I stood there above her on the hillside, boots planted firmly in the snow, scarf cracking like a stock-whip in the subzero wind, and looked down at her gasping toiling figure as she hauled herself along. I curled my lip as well as I could in the cold, and said, "How can you stand to be so out of condition? Doesn't it make you feel terribly *helpless*?"

When she got her breath she answered, reasonably enough, "Shut up."

I strode on, Diana the Huntress, Amazon, Valkyrie, spirit of youth, health, strength, freedom.

And the next day I whistled while cleaning the cat's pan. I had risen like the phoenix, not just because I felt strong and capable, but because I felt stronger and more capable than somebody else. This isn't a nice character trait, but apparently our identity, our sense of ourselves, rests in comparisons. How shall we feel brave and capable unless we've been visiting the weak and helpless? Therein, of course, lies one of the subtler problems of living alone, and one of our causes of gloom: we compare with no one, and cast no reflection on the air.

Another cause is the shortage of events. Without the quarrels and crises and frictions and plans of other people, life can smooth out into barely perceptible patterns.

Events that happened to us alone, our days and movements, lose their urgency because they went unrecorded, maybe unmentioned. Nobody else noticed; perhaps nothing happened after all, or mattered. A funny thing happened on our way to somewhere, but if there's no one to laugh, was it funny? Was it even real?

Monotony, as Burton keeps telling us, breeds depression.

We don't laugh enough, either. Laughing is said to be one of our most therapeutic habits, bringing almost mystical benefits in mental and physical health, expelling some subtle toxin from the lungs and jarring the brain's chemistry into healthy balance. All alone here, it's hard to work up a good hearty laugh. Sometimes days or weeks go by without one, unless we work in a merry office or are lucky enough to have funny friends. Are we kings, that we can hire a live-in jester with cap and bells? Still, we must keep an eye out for the occasional laugh; choose comedy, avoid depressants.

Even the quiet smile helps, I'm told. Even a smile we don't really feel, just the movement of the facial muscles, triggers a cheerful feedback to the brain. Smiling alone is easier than laughing. Smile at the mirror, smile at our morning coffee. Simpleminded therapy, perhaps, but affordable, and there's no one to jeer at us.

Solitary drinking as therapy for depression is disrecommended by the authorities. Boswell, in his *London Journal*, says his mentor, Dr. Johnson, "advised me to have constant occupation of mind, to take a great deal of exercise and live moderately; especially to shun drinking at night. 'Melancholy people,' said he, 'are apt to fly to intemperance, which gives a momentary relief but sinks the soul much lower in misery.' "

Alcohol in general has been under a cloud lately, in accordance with our mania for perfect health and total fitness, and this has put a damper on casual social life. Once, friends and new acquaintances could be asked to drop over for a drink. Nothing was expected of the hostess but a supply of drink, a bowl of potato chips, and a dip made of sour cream and onion soup mix. Then in the eighties strong drink and sour cream came to be considered unwholesome and were replaced by wine and squares of cheese on toothpicks. After a while everyone got pretty fed up with this fare, and cheese turned out to be poisonously full of cholesterol. Easy gatherings withered. Inviting folks over, or joining them after work, for diet soda and carrot sticks just doesn't have the same impact.

A few of us still like an occasional drink. More solitary men than solitary women go to bars for it, and for the company; they can't be said to be drinking alone, even if there's no one else there but the bartender, and they probably find the effects less depressing than at home.

Uncoupled women may go in pairs or groups to bars after work, but older or less gregarious ones go home, perhaps to have a drink there.

One of the paths to solitary drinking is time. Living alone leaves blank patches of time, odd shapeless chunks of time that familied people spend taking care of their families or simply hanging out with them, which can take up a string of evening and weekend hours. Especially for the newly widowed or divorced, these empty patches feel awkward. They can weigh a hundred pounds an hour. We hurry home after work, not pausing to window-shop or chat, because home, by definition, needs us to be there. We turn the key quickly and let ourselves in, and feel the empty air on our faces. We sit down and wait to be needed. Surely, if we sit long enough, someone will want us to run a load of wash or pick him up at the airport or drive them to the movies.

Nobody does.

The personal use of a piece of time, for those unused to it, takes learning. In the meantime, what's to be done with this strange blind empty-handed hour that swells around us like The Blob (where *is* everybody?) but sit and have a drink while we wait to be told what to do next? If we went out for a walk or to shop, the invisible someone might need us while we were out. The drink keeps us here, available and waiting, ready to leap up and look for someone's track shoes at a moment's notice.

The problem then arises: when do we stop drinking, and why? No one does come demanding to be driven somewhere; no one wants dinner. No one even gives a damn whether *we* eat dinner. There's no pressing reason not to go on drinking until we run out of things to drink, including the vanilla extract.

The only advantage of having gone all the way through to the vanilla the night before is that while you're struggling up through the brown fog of the next morning you feel so foolish and guilty that you make amends to the gods by scrubbing the kitchen floor, calling your mother, and sewing buttons on everything.

The disadvantages include creeping depression.

The first drink is solace, a comforting hand on the brow. It was a tough day at the office. We deserve to unwind; we deserve a hug. There's no one around to say we were good, we did a swell job, or that we screwed up but it doesn't matter, forget it. Only the bottle will tell us.

We sit there with our drink as if we were enjoying a pre-dinner chat with a significant other, but we aren't. We're all by ourselves, and we might as well have another drink before we start dinner.

If we keep it up, the gentle reassurance of the drink changes character and works its way into the brain like a worm, burrowing among lost loves and half-forgotten wounds. The grandmother who sang us to sleep will never sing again. The love of our life left nothing behind but a sprung tennis racket and a note saying he was going to Baja to think about whales. The things we have lost are lost forever and the mistakes we made were permanent and can never be repaired.

After another drink the ghosts in the room turn hostile. We remember things best forgotten, like our parents' errors. They punished us for crimes that weren't our fault. They gave someone else what was rightfully ours. They loved our sister more. We were good and tried hard but it was no use. We spent days choosing a birthday present and they took it back to the store.

At this point, having no one else around on whom to vent this paranoia, some of us take pen in hand and write to tell the people who wronged us what a pack of stinkers they were. Luckily we seldom manage to locate a stamp and an envelope, and the address, and put on our coats and go out to find a mailbox. In the morning, blushing, we can throw the letters away.

On the other hand, if we pick up the phone to pour out our grievances, we're in for serious embarrassment.

Friendly alcohol has turned against us, and if we can't

keep it in hand we're going to have to sign on with AA. Besides, alone here, we need to stay alert and avoid substances that cloud the mind; we have no backup, and if we forget to lock the door at night, who will remember?

The next day's well-earned shame is worse for us than the attendant hangover, and leads to depression, which wears a trail for itself in the head and finds it easier to come back next time.

Better to busy ourselves after work with regular activities, a class, some volunteer usefulness, or even, if all else fails, jogging. At home, rather than sitting there with the bottle, marshal a row of tasks to go along with the drink, something physical that needs concentration—a jigsaw puzzle, refinishing the coffee table, patching all the worn spots in an old quilt, organizing recipes, repotting the houseplants, shining all the shoes, waxing all the floors, polishing the silver, or straightening the bureau drawers. Concentrate; use our hands. When we're finished, make dinner.

It's better, of course, to drink with a friend, a friend conveniently located and of similar habits, as long as the friend has only a casual and cheerful interest in drink. If we spend the cocktail hour with heavy, gloomy drinkers, we may find ourselves keeping up with them. Sharing our troubles along with our bottle, we find the world getting blacker faster. Just because misery loves company doesn't make it therapeutic. Any little depressant we may have forgotten about, our friend is sure to remember, until we both dissolve in boozy tears.

A drinking companion should be merry, stalwart, temperate, and easily bored by other people's complaints. Burton says, "Many and sundry are the means which Philosophers and Physicians have prescribed to exhilarate a sorrowful heart, to divert those fixed and intent cares and meditations, which in this malady [melancholy] do so much to offend; but in my judgment none so present, none so powerful, none so apposite, as a cup of strong drink, mirth, musick, and merry company. Wine and Musick rejoice the heart."

For those with a tendency to sit too long alone with their own bottle, going out for a drink has the advantage of being more self-limiting, along with the pleasures of faces to see and different walls.

Ray Oldenburg, in his recent book, *The Great Good Place: Cafes, Coffee Shops, Community Centers, Beauty Parlors, General Stores, Bars, Hangouts, and How They Get You Through the Day*, laments the decline in America of what he calls "third places," neither work nor home, where people gather. They gather to meet friends or talk to strangers, maybe even encounter neighbors they'd otherwise never meet, and hang around chatting and socializing or eavesdropping. Oldenburg feels these places are essential to family and community life and the political process; they're even more necessary to us, alone in quiet motionless apartments. They're vanishing, these loitering places, leaving only the impersonal, commercially planned shopping mall. Merchandise is all around us, but talk has become the rarest of commodities, and for talky people from talky families the unanswering furniture of our silent rooms can seem like a punishment. We need a place in which to talk, and buttonholing strangers in shopping malls is unacceptable.

If we're lucky enough to live near a friendly neighborhood bar we should take advantage of its warmth, and never mind what our mother would say. If not, even the blue-glass chill of bars attached to hotels and expensive restaurants is an improvement over the kitchen table. Making it clear by our deportment that we aren't looking for a quick tumble with strangers—unless, of course, we are—we can order a drink and sit there looking alert and pleasant and open to conversation. (Nondrinkers are free to order other things designed to look like real drinks, such as Virgin Marys. A generous tip will compensate the bartender for the lower price.) Maybe the bartender, intent on television, will be the only other person there, or maybe the place will fill up with upwardly mobile law clerks, in which case we can try someplace else.

In a neighborhood bar, we will come to recognize the

regulars, and they will at the very least nod at us when we come in, recognizing us in turn, and this small spark of contact has its comforts. In hotel bars, there's likely to be a lone man, in town on business, lonely rather than lustful. He misses his family and carries snapshots of his kids. One or the other of us will mention the weather. Probably he will offer to buy us our second drink. Politely we will discuss the decline of public education or the high cost of heating oil. Then we thank him for the drink and go home to make dinner or go to bed, depending on the hour. This isn't what Pepys would call fun, exactly, and it isn't a prospective romance, but at least we've been out somewhere and spoken to someone.

In other times and places, public drinking houses were a more festive source of solace, of what E. B. White called "the golden companionship of the tavern," and of what Dr. Johnson meant when he called the pub the throne of human felicity. Ours are poor thin imitations now, but being alone is about compromise, and adjustments, and wringing all possible nourishment from the food we find at hand.

We need to stay on guard against that which lowers the depression threshold and invites it in—monotony, the sense of helplessness, discouragement, drink, loneliness, boredom. (I've even heard that spending more than a couple of hours in front of the television set can induce a mild, transient depression all by itself.)

Once it wraps us in its damp gray arms, depression is hard to shake. Better to keep our lives stirred up and well populated, even a bit stressful, so it can't get a foothold—rather like a farm wife flapping her apron and waving her arms to keep the crows from settling onto the cornfield.

Chapter 10

Anxiety

Like one that on a lonesome road
Doth walk in fear and dread,
and having once turned round, walks on,
And turns no more his head;
Because he knows a frightful fiend
Doth close behind him tread.

—COLERIDGE

In the beginning was the group, the tribe, the clan, the extended family. Shivering, vulnerable, we crawled together into the same cave and slept in a heap, sharing each other's fleas and twitching with the same dreams about saber-tooth tigers. If there were outcasts, they didn't live long.

As things got safer, an occasional hermit would elect to go live in the desert, alone in a fringe-area cave. Probably the children were scared of him or her, but the superstitious might carry over a gourd-full of mashed roots anyway, just in case the loner was responding to a mystic message instead of an uncontrollable blip in the brain. (Certified saints were fed by supernatural means, their breakfast often conveyed by wild animals, or ravens, bringing whatever ravens consider breakfast.) The very fact that these people lived alone, unmarried, unattached to the web of society, was evidence of saintliness, or something equally alarming.

As our tribes grew rich and powerful, housing improved to the point where families could live alone together, just husband and wife and children and servants and granny and the cats and dogs and horses and maybe a bachelor uncle who thought he was the Emperor Augustus.

Then we got even richer, at least in favored areas. We could lavish walls and roofs and floor space on a single person, alone at table and in bed, physically disconnected from the rest of the tribe. Enormous numbers of us now live this way by choice, dodging what's called "commitment," preferring independence and the unshared salary. Others of us are sorry to be here but can't seem to find a way out of it, or company to join us in it. We were raised to believe that, at least after college age, living quarters should be shared only with those we love, not just with a heap of similar creatures on the floor of the cave. We're waiting.

Once in a while, the isolation is bound to feel dangerous. Civilization isn't so old that we can't still hear, from time to time, something snuffling around the mouth of the cave, and we wonder where everyone went. Sometimes a twig snaps out there. We're still just as soft and naked, flightless, clumsy, clawless and blunt-toothed as we were in earlier times, and now we have no one but our solitary selves, lying here wide-eyed and listening to the dark.

Normal worrying is a natural safeguard, and we need it. The tigers out there are real, just as plentiful as ever, and better armed than they used to be. In olden times, honest folk might lie awake worrying about the bags of gold in the basement, but they had it easy, comparatively speaking. Most of us now would gladly hand over the gold to anyone who asked politely, and when robbed, we rejoice that only the appliances are missing and we ourselves were out at the time. The old, relatively kindly custom of making off in peace with the valuables has given way to taking the valuables and then beating or murdering their former owner. In the streets, people whose wallets hold less than fifty dollars get killed by the disappointed mugger, and those with more may get killed just on general principles. That isn't mere covetousness stalking the streets out there; it's a downright uncharitable attitude, backed by sophisticated firepower, and we do well to worry.

People alone naturally worry more. Life simply seems chancier when you walk through it exposed on all four sides, and any enterprise, from moving to a new apartment to flying a plane, carries more anxious freight when we do it by ourselves. Besides, people in families can talk it over, and get a bit of reassurance or a derisive horse-laugh, and then forget about it. People alone can sit in a room worrying till their ulcers bleed and their hair falls out, and no one's there to stop them.

When something frightening does happen, and sometimes even when it doesn't, we can topple over the edge into panic. Anxiety begins to cling to our lives, even by daylight. Nameless dangers bloom in the brain and hide in the closets. We stop being afraid of *something* and become simply afraid. As Daniel Defoe said in *Journal of the Plague Year*, "Nobody can account for the possession of fear when it takes hold of the mind." The locks on the doors and windows multiply until it takes us twenty minutes to bolt ourselves in for the night, and in case of fire we shall surely cook before we can escape, but still the fear seeps in through the keyholes and up through the floor. The absence of other people in the room has created a vacuum, into which murderers will surely be sucked.

We sit there listening to the quiet, hanging like a curtain behind the music on the tape, and presently we turn off the music in order to listen more closely. All the neighbors must have gone out to parties. Or perhaps they've simply been murdered by someone who is still in the building, padding softly along the halls, droplets of blood soaking into the carpet from the knife in his hand. We hear no television, no voices, only a little traffic too far away to hear us if we screamed.

Sensibly, we call a friend for a chat. The phone company keeps telling us how good this is, how it's just like touching someone. It isn't, though. The voice without flesh is consoling while it lasts, but as soon as the connection's broken it evaporates without a trace. Perhaps it wasn't even a friend at all. Perhaps it was a recording, or some new trick the phone people will add to our bill. Sometimes other voices call us from out there, often wanting someone else. I have friends who assume that all wrong numbers are burglars, though it baffles me why a burglar would call me and ask for Sue, and if that's the closest he's going to come it's fine with me. I get calls for a doctor with an Italian name I can't catch and, between two and four in the morning, for various women sought by gentlemen too deep in their cups to remember the number, though not to argue. They sound too unsteady to be dangerous, but they aren't much company. And always I get calls from people selling things, who invariably start by asking how I am this evening; one of these days I'll think of the right answer. They aren't company either.

For evening anxieties, any other person around would be a help, even a small child. Actually a small child might be best. It would make us feel older, stronger, more capable; we would go in and turn off its television, tuck the blanket under its chin, and say, "See you in the morning," and then go back and read in peace, our place in the scheme of things established, protector of the small. And what crazed killer would have the heart to break into a house where a child lies sleeping?

Somewhere down the hall a door closes softly. Too softly, meaning the killer has finished off Wendy and Linda, and we're next.

"As timid as a lone woman with her silver spoons," Thoreau sneered. Oh well, we're not alone, anyway. A study of sea gull behavior shows that the unmated females dither on the edges of the colony, skittish and shy, nervous and unconfident, and jump away when anyone moves near them.

It's this damned helplessness, being alone and female. It's one of life's primal lessons, almost impossible and probably dangerous to unlearn. We feel like helpless potential victims because we are helpless potential victims, now in adulthood as previously on the playground.

Morally and intellectually I disapprove of guns. It's too easy to do damage with a gun; even quite small children can kill with them, and do. The damage one does with a gun apparently feels morally neutral and remote, because of its mechanical, long-distance action; a far cleaner feeling than, say, strangling one's victim face to face. The gun, not one's hands, does the dirty work. People shouldn't be allowed to have guns, and when surrounded by city, I want one badly.

I saw too many Westerns as a child and developed a kind of holstered penis envy: the men had guns. The ladies fainted and had to be dragged to safety behind the stagecoach while the gents popped away at each other, and the good gent won. That was how, aside from the white hat, you could tell he was good—he shot the bad guy.

Marksmanship, at the Saturday matinee, was the supreme test of virtue, and it was reserved almost exclusively for men, women's virtue being reserved for chastity. Only Annie Oakley and Melanie Wilkes stood behind their smoking pistols; the rest of us had to look for a good man with a gun to save us from the bad men with guns. Now we're supposed to try to get to a phone and dial the police emergency number, and pray somebody answers it in time to send a good man with a gun to save us from the black-hat who is even now climbing our fire escape.

I'd really rather shoot him myself. I want to be able to hurt someone who wants to hurt me. Deep in my soul, I *mind* the unlikelihood of saving myself from harm. It bothers me in dark streets and lonely farmhouses and well-bolted apartments. It seems unfair.

For a few pipe-dreaming, high-flying feminist years, back in the late seventies, women were encouraged to take classes in self-defense. Learn Oriental tricks by which we could spin a two-hundred-pound armed male around our heads and break his back on the pavement. The notion faded and the ads and television commercials tiptoed away, possibly after a lot of women got more seriously hurt than they otherwise would have been.

Equal pay for equal work is a possibility, if a remote one; self-defense is a dream. I know perfectly well I can't subdue an attacker by poking my thumbs in his eyes and my knee in his groin. It's just going to make him madder. And thirty years from now when I have arthritis and need to hobble off to the grocery store, I'll be a pushover for any passing five-year-old.

When did we lay down our arms? Surely humans of both sexes once needed weapons, the thrown rock, the sharpened stick; weren't we in equal danger? At some point we stopped using them, turned them over to the men, who promised to protect us whenever they happened to be in the neighborhood. We even gave up the muscles and the confidence necessary to use them. Some of us now are trying to recover the muscles, but face it, they'll never be a man's muscles; we can't even arm-wrestle a man.

The lady duck, lady turtle, rattlesnake, and raccoon are as well armed and defended as the males, and I've seen a five-pound mother cat chase Dobermans out of her yard and send them home howling. Why not us?

I want a gun. And a carry permit. The more helpless I feel, the more clearly I can see it; it lives in the night-stand drawer by the bed and I know it's there. When I hear a funny noise at night, I will take it out, flip off the safety catch, and lie there holding it, armed, not a mere quivering lump in the bed waiting to be raped and shot.

If I could, just once, say to a full-grown man, "Don't move, I've got you covered," it would ward off the next three bouts of depression. "Raise your hands over your head and back up against the wall," I would say, and my whole life would take a turn for the happier.

Yes, I know, I know, I would shoot the cat, or the UPS man, or my own foot, or my own shadow in the mirror. I don't care. The revolver in my nightstand drawer would make me whistle in the street, and complain to waiters, and ask for a raise. Never mind the penises, I want a gun.

Probably I will never get one. Probably I'll go right

on apologizing to waiters, too, and listening for footsteps in the night.

Of course it's irrational, to feel anxious and vulnerable just because of being female and alone, in these days of impetuous and mindless crime. The only person I know who was actually robbed, beaten, and left for dead in his own apartment is a healthy man in his late twenties. I doubt if he'll ever recover. A year later he still prowls his rooms, checking locks, pulling down shades, sneaking up on his own bathroom and jerking the door open, shining a flashlight into closets. Perhaps it was harder on him than it would have been on me; men don't expect it.

Expecting harm gives us insomnia and ulcers. Statistically, we may be in more danger from anxiety than from burglars.

Maybe we should pack up everything and move to someplace safer. Someplace where the most recent crime, years ago now, was a stolen bicycle, later returned undamaged by the anonymous thief. There will be little to do there for solitary people, after the Wednesday-night bingo game, and the commute will add hours to our working day, but we won't hear sirens in the night.

Unfortunately when we pack, we pack the wretched panic too, and sooner or later it leaks out of the box. We can sit peacefully in the cabin in the harmless hill country, and suddenly the cat wakes up and stares alertly at the black window. Outside a twig snaps under a foot. The heart stops and then lurches, and we sit clenched rigid with terror, unable to move, unable to reach out, even, and turn on the television for company, because if we do an announcer will say, "We interrupt this program to bring you an urgent bulletin. The escaped killer is in your neighborhood. He has crossed the lawn and even now crouches under your windowsill, hidden in the dark rhododendrons, waiting." There we sit, shaking silently, until long after the cat has gone back to sleep and the raccoon moved on to investigate the garbage can.

For those who live alone, fear can come bulging out in odd places, as if we were buttoned crookedly into our emotional clothes. Simply knowing we're being an idiot is no help; terror has no trouble sitting side by side with common sense. It lives in the murky bottom of the brain's Loch Ness, untouched by reason.

It can metastasize. Something triggers it—a car accident, a lump in the breast, coming home to find the window open and the VCR missing—and then it moves in and sets up housekeeping in our heads. The fender was easily fixed, the lump benign, the VCR replaced, and we're still jumping out of our skins. It's gone systemic on us. Our wallet was stolen, so we're afraid to answer the phone. Walk down the stairs. Open the electric bill. Once called the jitters, or hoo-has, this state is now dignified as

Post-Traumatic Stress Syndrome by the psychologists. They allow us up to ninety days to recover from it, depending on the severity of the trauma. (They want it to have been a genuine trauma, too, not a "perceived" threat, though for the life of me I can't see what difference it makes whether the knife in his hand was real or just a harmonica, or a spoon, or light glancing off a ring: panic is panic.)

Ninety days is a long time to stay scared, and I don't know how they arrived at this time span, but I suppose it's a comfort to think, This too shall pass, like the common cold. If it doesn't, we're supposed to take it, like the cold, to professional helpers.

We can get courage pills from the doctor, and in their heyday a few years back, many a big strong successful man wouldn't dream of making a speech, getting on a plane, or even going to a meeting without his Valium. Pills are nice but habit-forming, and perhaps slightly shameful except in emergencies.

We can take the humdrum little steps to make ourselves feel safer: wear our seat belts, go for mammograms, check the batteries in the smoke detector. Avoid rubbing our noses in the world's dangers, real or imaginary: late-night movies in which someone's alone in her apartment, and then there's a shot of feet walking down the hall, and the bolt on the inside of her door slides back, and then we see her squeezed into the corner of her bed with her hair in a mess, clutching the sheets and screaming.

Maybe we should all chip in and have a more encouraging video made, in which the lady leaps out of bed and throws a hammerlock on the villain and tosses him through the nearest window twenty-two floors to the street. Or knocks him out cold with the bedside lamp. Or bursts into peals of laughter and tells him his fly's unzipped, and the cur slinks away in shame.

Also avoid books in which supernatural bloody handprints feel their way up the stairwell, tabby cats grow fangs at midnight, and a hand with talons reaches out through a cracked mirror. If addicted to the genre, stop reading well before bedtime. By the bed, we can keep a jumble of gentle, amiable, lighthearted books. Books about English village life, fishing trips, Colonial gardens, the châteaux of the Loire, bird-watching, quilt-making, wine-tasting, seaside holidays in 1910, Jane Austen, biking tours of the New England churches, the sex life of the butterfly. Half an hour with one of these before sleep—if we can stay awake that long—and the gentle bucolic considerations sink down inside the head. If, later, we find ourselves lying stiff-legged in bed wishing the air conditioner would shut up so we could listen more closely to what might be footsteps, then we turn on the light and read some more, paying attention, so all those vineyards and church steeples and trout ponds don't evaporate before we can sleep.

Reading is a thin substitute for the warmth and quiet breathing of our true love, but it's more easily available.

Sometimes, of course, these homemade preventive measures don't work. Anxiety moves in, and trots along with us wherever we go, fading in and out like the possibility of toothache. Our dreams, when we can sleep, are disagreeable, and the steering wheel of our car threatens to come off in our hands. Even our junk mail looks sinister. So do bridges. Tunnels. Suitcases.

Three people I know, young enough to retain the option, simply moved back home with parents or widowed mothers. Most of us have relatives of some sort, preferably safe, stuffy relatives, and sometimes a long visit with them, overdosing on security, can restore our perspective.

The ideal relatives would be an aunt and uncle living in a sleepy little town where, after nine in the evening, nothing is stirring, not even a burglar. In their spare bedroom no nameless, faceless monsters ever lurked; the wallpaper frightened them off. This perfect couple would have been married for twenty-seven years, and for the past twenty-five have been having the same arguments, in the same words, about each other's table manners and the causes of the common cold. We are asked nightly over dinner about our marriage plans and whatever happened to that nice boy we knew in college? She criticizes the neighbors; he's in favor of nuking the rest of the world before it nukes us. Both feel that AIDS is divine retribution. Each tells us privately that the other is going deaf, making him/her even harder to live with. Probably they're both right; the television stays tuned to the top of its shout night and day.

By Thursday the loving warmth of safety will feel like dungeon walls covered with greeny-slime, and we cut our visit short in favor of any possible danger home might hold.

We flee back to the scene of our lonely terrors and lo, the sun is shining in and our friendly furniture is glad to see us. What could we possibly have feared in this kindly room?

Oh, all sorts of things.

Joan, a pretty redhead I knew who lived alone in Manhattan, was found dead of skull injuries in her bathtub, without evidence of foul play. The coroner did not commit himself as to whether she could have been saved if she hadn't been alone, but somehow we all took it for granted. We all said, "It really makes you think twice about living alone." One semidetached couple in our circle got married a month later; Joan's name kept coming up at the wedding, like an accident narrowly averted.

Joan had the kind of freewheeling job where people trickle into the office at any old hour before noon. If she'd been living with someone, and this imaginary helpful husband or lover had a more scheduled job, she would have let him shower first while she made breakfast. Chances are she would then have eaten breakfast with him in her bathrobe. She would have kissed him goodbye, and *then* she would have gone off to slip in the shower, nine long hours before he came home to help.

It can seem more precarious than it is, this being alone. We imagine people in families as living protected by loving arms at all times. They aren't. Nobody is. People die of heart attacks inches away from their sleeping loved ones, and slip in the shower with nobody home but a terrified two-year-old. It's well to get away from the broody sense of being singled out for the special attentions of mortality because of our solitude. Families can be lovely but they aren't safety; if the bell tolls for thee, not even your closest relatives can be sent to muffle it.

Solitude, if we take ordinary precautions, is really only marginally more dangerous than life with people. It just feels that way occasionally, an outgrowth of loneliness, impotence, and too much time to think.

Walk in the light. Take taxis. Lock the car doors while driving and the house doors while sleeping. Go for checkups. Stay cheerful. Have friends. Keep in touch.

A group of women I know have set up a signal system, and call each other to report in at a certain hour, but this presupposes an orderly sort of life. If you've sworn to check in with Betsy at ten every night, and forget and go to a party instead, it's embarrassing to come home and find your premises swarming with police and the rescue squad.

Know your neighbors. Don't smoke in bed. Drive defensively.

A friend of mine worries that something will happen to her, all alone there, and her dog and cat will starve before she's found. She has a clear vision of this, of them whining sadly and pawing at her stiffened body at the foot of the stairs, and their dishes empty, their water bowl dry. This is the kind of vision we should try to avoid.

Sane precautions help keep the hounds at bay when we're feeling sane, but they wilt when faced with the hardcore paranoia, the irrational sense of fragility that seizes after an obscene phone call or a death in the family and takes up residence just below the breastbone, causing us to feel at the mercy of any old disaster that wants to stroll into our lives. Against this, we need to shore up the interior cockiness. Courage is power. It won't save us from the actual mugger or the actual accident, but neither will panic. Besides, panic's humiliating.

Panic and courage both reinforce themselves. If we're afraid to go out after dark this month, next month we'll be afraid to go to work in the morning. And if we walk to the edge of the roof and lean over and look down, tomorrow we'll be able to take flying lessons. Or, as Shakespeare said, "Out of this nettle, danger, we pluck this flower, safety." Working slowly, with small risks taken and survived, we can build up the sense of competence that fends off fright.

Take money out of the savings account and put it in the stock market. Make eye contact in the streets. Criticize taxi drivers. Turn down boring invitations. Complain to the boss. Buy a motorcycle. Join a rock-climbing club. Take advanced riding lessons. Join a protest group and get arrested. Run for city council. Sue the landlord. Fall in love. Quit the job. Jaywalk. Exceed the speed limit. Make a speech. Try out for the drama group. Find something that makes our palms sweat at the very thought, and go and do it.

Fear is a rabbit on the road, paralyzed in the glare of the headlights. Courage is being the driver.

What are we, then, O daughters of the pioneers, a pack of rabbits?

In the meantime, while we're still assembling our courage brick by brick, we need to treat our fears with tolerance. Sometimes a decent night's sleep means more to us than self-respect, and when we can't subdue the panic, there's nothing shameful in giving in and running away. We can get up and dress and go to find a friend's warm couch to burrow into, re-creating the primal cave; we can listen to friendly breathing in the night.

Chapter 11

Alternatives

Afoot and lighthearted I take to the
    open road,
Healthy, free, the world before me,
The long brown path before me,
    leading wherever I choose.

—WALT WHITMAN

After we've done all we can to make ourselves comfortable, here we still are on our own, and sometimes at ease with our condition and sometimes restless enough to call 800 numbers and talk to their recordings. Sometimes our lives feel full and nourishing, and sometimes we wonder.

To be half of a loving couple is a great source of joy and strength for humans and quite a few other animals, including birds, but looking around among our friends and relations we can see that it's not all that common. Our married friends have troubles too, and twice the opportunity to suffer, having another person around to inflict suffering. Men are better off emotionally when married, but married women report 20 percent more depression than single women, and three times the rate of severe neurosis. Just the same, we sometimes feel any intimate relationship, however flawed or even degrading, would be worth the price of not standing here outside the lighted windows, with the wind rising on all sides, blowing through the hollow marrow of our bones until they peep like flutes.

Sometimes we feel our solitary state must reflect some failing of our own. Maybe we aren't as kind and good or as attractive as we're expected to be, or maybe we made an awful mistake somewhere, preventable but not mendable, that brought down on our heads this most ancient of punishments, solitary confinement. The popular psychologists keep urging us to take steps—usually twelve steps, the mystic number of most self-improvement programs—to reform our lives and find happiness. The implication is that whatever our problems, they're our own fault. The books don't believe we might be here, not because of our personal inadequacies, but from simple bad luck. This is damned unfair. Luck is not superstition; luck, good and bad, is a vital factor in all life stories, and denying it puts an undeserved strain on the individual. This isn't to say we should lie down on the job of improving our lives, only that there's no use either blaming or praising ourselves for the mysterious workings of fortune.

If we aren't half of a loving couple—and at least for the moment we aren't—then the next best thing is to spend as much time as possible in the company of people we love. When this isn't possible, we can fall back on ordinary, unloved people, just for their ordinary human faces and voices, who just might, in time, upgrade themselves. Work is what gives us our bread and butter, stability and place in the world, but love keeps us human. Any old kind of love.

We can leave ourselves open to loving some of the people we already know. Most of my single friends spend a lot of time and energy trying to meet new people, as if people not yet met were certain to be an improvement over the ones they know now, or as if sheer quantity were somehow the point, as if a hundred, or five hundred, names and phone numbers give more ballast and bottom to life than ten. These seekers go through their days like guests at a perpetual cocktail party, introducing themselves over and over, searching for more and better or somehow different humans. Not even the prince or princess, necessarily. People, new people, from whom they expect some nameless, elusive reward.

We check our mail in the same spirit, when we get home from work. Riffle through the pile, and all those magazines we subscribe to, because magazines are different from books; they come to our door like friends bearing messages. But where is the mail we were looking for, and what would it look like if it came? It's a letter from a stranger, probably. Somebody new. But which new people do we want, and what would we do with them if we found them? What will they do for us?

Maybe the people we know already are good enough, or would be if we were paying close enough attention. Consider the solitary prisoners of old who had a favorite rat for a friend, and found his bright eyes and cheerful whiskers consoling.

We might find a friend we love well enough to endure in daily life, and share living quarters with. This is a tricky proposition, of course, and longstanding friendships have crashed on those rocks. We're past the flexibility of dormitory days; we're grown up and have our own ways and habits.

I tried it, and moved into the house of a dear friend, after we were both divorced, and moved out again nine months later, our friendship temporarily crippled. It was her house, not mine. I'd been a happy guest there often, but a housemate is not a guest, and in someone else's house she's not a first-class citizen, either. Her opinions on laundry and floor-waxing and flea-killing and dish-drying and the proper way to cook eggs are irrelevant, even unwelcome. Ownership matters. There are land-lords and there are tenants, and always have been.

An equally shared house or apartment is easier; compromises can be made. With three or four people inhabiting quarters together, the opportunities for friction multiply but the pressure on the relationships is lighter. In metropolitan areas where rents keep rising, along with the population of the unattached, group houses and shares are a rapidly growing trend and the classified ads for roommates fill column after column. Total strangers answer the ads, and move in with their baggage and quirks and bathroom habits, to become either intimate members of a supportive family or temporary nuisances passing through.

When it comes to house-sharing, it may be that personal affection is less important than temperament. (Is it possible that, in the long run, this is true of marriage too?) Friend or stranger, the person who leaves wet towels on the couch and banana peels in the sink is more than a passing irritation to the person who wants the lamp shade seams turned to the wall and the toilet paper flap hanging down on the inside, not the outside. Matters like this, alas, run deeper than fondness, and there's no forgiving them. The laid-back and the uptight, the talky and the reserved, the organizer and the slob, the optimist and the cynic, are all going to strike sparks. Opposites attract, people keep telling us, but this is no consolation when you're cleaning the kitchen together.

My sister and brother and two friends of theirs shared a house, a house with room enough to keep their elbows disentangled and even shelter overnight guests. It worked happily for a couple of years, a long time for these arrangements. Resentments flared up and faded away, as in marriages. Someone's dog had incurable fleas; someone's cat shed abundantly in the spring; someone's cockatiel would fly around the kitchen and shit on the toast. But often on a weekend the group went out on adventures together, and meals and groceries were entirely spontaneous. Anyone who felt like cooking would shop, cook, and share with anyone around. Two of the group kept later hours than the others and often cooked after midnight; their leftovers were found and eaten by early risers the next day.

The idyll crashed, as they tend to do. One of the group fell in love, and a fifth party moved in. The happy couple kept their door shut, and tried to live as if they were alone, possibly on a mountaintop in Tibet. They weren't alone, though, and the intrusions of other people rubbed their nerves. The others, left out, felt the couple as an indigestible lump in their midst. Tempers flared more frequently, and the communal refrigerator and food shelves multiplied into several private refrigerators and separate caches of cereal and canned goods. Presently all hands began to make plans to move.

Group houses are fragile. Because everyone is free to leave at once and forever, the loose arrangement calls for even more goodwill and determined tact than a house of kin. Kinship families traditionally have a leader who decides when to turn the air conditioner on and off, while the rest bake or shiver accordingly, complaining but helpless, as in a monarchy. Democracies are volatile, delicate, inefficient, fractious. Trivial matters like who ate Janet's yogurt, and whether aspirin and toothpaste are common property or individual possessions, can snowball into war.

Pets and children complicate the matter infinitely, as do lovers who spend the weekend, eating freely, using countless gallons of hot water, and hogging the Sunday papers. The division of labor is complicated; in mixed-sex households, males may elect to do simple, weekly tasks like carrying out the trash and mowing the lawn, while the females get stuck with nightly kitchen drudgery, brooding dangerously. I knew a happy household that fractured over a presidential election; during the home-stretch of the campaign it was found that the differences

between liberals and conservatives are deep and irrecon-
cilable and extend to such domestic matters as how to
cover leftovers and where to leave wet boots.

Suddenly what had felt like dear and loving family
atomizes in an afternoon, leaving the lease-signer holding
the bag, forced to bring in strangers, perhaps with bizarre
vices, from a classified ad.

Group houses, being new on the scene, are an experimental art form and open to infinite interpretation. Ideally, a stable arrangement can give us something that feels
like home. People there will listen to our comments and
opinions, triumphs and complaints, and offer us theirs—
which keeps us from focusing too closely on our own. It
can validate and shape our days.

Even the most practical, impersonal arrangement,
worked out purely to share rent, can have advantages that
offset the loss of privacy. Privacy may be overvalued; it
certainly isn't a concept widespread among the human
race, and we may not need it as much as we think we do.
Maybe we equally need the sound of another human being brushing its teeth and cursing the toaster. Maybe a
door to close occasionally and a bed of our own is really
all the private space we require. People in group houses
develop intimate relationships with their beds. The bed
is their island turf, nest, cave, sanctuary, and they pile it
with novels and pillows, take naps, write letters, eat pop-

corn, watch television, and entertain friends on it. It's the private property of the common house.

Beyond it, outside the bedroom door, there's someone to talk to. Someone to help you start your car or button your blouse up the back.

Another consideration in favor of the group house is its openness to human variety. Since it's only a shelter arrangement, not an emotional commitment, it can take in male and female, old and young, gay and straight, artist and accountant, and as long as the temperaments don't clash too sharply the differences don't matter. Variety gives our lives more texture and flavor. Left to our own devices we tend to assemble friends too much like ourselves, and can find that we're in contact only with, say, divorced women within five years of our age who play bridge. Or we cultivate only people suitable by age and inclination and social level to be romantic possibilities. This is a waste of our freedoms, one of which is the freedom to make strange friends and visit unfamiliar lives. Single life should be experimental in nature and open to accidents. Some accidents are happy ones.

If we already have our own quarters, we can consider taking in friends and relations. One divorced man I know keeps on his premises a son in his twenties, the son's girlfriend, the son's best friend and *his* girlfriend, and seems wonderfully happy in his new role as dorm master.

My friend Linda managed to hold on to the house after her divorce, and rents the guest room to a succession of students and the underemployed. Some of these are cheerful and helpful, some dour and untidy. At best, they're company, and even at worst they're the sound of a shower running, a door opening and closing; reassurance that the rest of the human race hasn't packed up and moved to Uranus in the night.

Not so long ago, the urban unmarried lived in boardinghouses, and there was something to be said for them. You never had to worry about what to make for dinner; dinner might be nasty, but it was effortless. You could hear the footsteps of other humans, chat in the hall if you were so minded, or retire to your room without hurting anyone's feelings. I'm not sure why they slid into such disrepute and more or less vanished. Perhaps they should be revived.

Whatever the options, the majority of us go on living in our separate apartments, apart, and this too has its advantages. Autonomy can be habit-forming, and there are pleasures like leaving the bathroom door open, a boon to the claustrophobic, and the simple economy of eating out of the saucepan to save the extra step and the extra dish.

Which brings us back, as each day brings us, to dinner. The other day I saw a classified ad in a community newspaper in rural Virginia, an area of farms and villages and few restaurants. A woman who described herself as a "pleasant lady," living near one of the villages, wished to be an occasional paying dinner guest with a private family. It's an ingenious thought, fraught with odd possibilities, maybe the beginning of a novel, but the string of lonely meals that finally forced the pleasant lady to pick up the phone and place that notice hardly bears thinking about.

Dining alone bothers us all far more than sleeping alone. Half the bananas turn black, the bread molds, the butter develops alien smells, and ambitious batches of chicken soup gather frost in the freezer or get fed to the garbage disposal. ("When I lived alone," says Anita, happily dicing carrots in a group house, "I did nothing but pitch food.") As we feed ourselves in solitude, a whitish gray fog gathers between us and the world's happenings, blotting us out. Invisibility threatens us. The eighteenth-century philosopher Bishop Berkeley said, "To be is to be perceived," and we might, just possibly, cease to exist while forking around in the Chinese take-out box for the last shrimp.

Back when everyone I knew was twenty-five years old and lived alone in one-room apartments in the city, a dinner group formed around the apartment with the largest kitchen. If you planned to eat there that night, in the afternoon you called to reserve your share. The volunteer cook/shopper, who worked an early schedule and left his office at four-thirty, shopped and cooked for the number of people expected, charging each mouth its percent of the grocery bill. Separate money for wine or martinis went in a coffee can on the refrigerator. In time the group heaved and shattered, married or moved away, but it had worked well for several years. (A fairer arrangement would have rotated the cooking, but our volunteer enjoyed the job. It filled in that awkward gray area between day and evening that haunts so many solitaries.)

We need a little ingenuity. New ways and attitudes. There are so many of us here; behind nearly a quarter of the closed doors in this country somebody lives alone. After we've been solitary for a while, we find that most of our friends are solitaries too, and we have separated ourselves from the mainstream. People in nuclear families begin to seem like a different tribe, carrying on their lives nearby but in different ceremonies and a different language.

In spite of this, however, many of us find our expectations still tethered to this neighboring clan. They're still the norm, in spite of their dwindling numbers. We're told that they, the American nuclear families, are the very flesh and blood of the nation's most cherished traditional values. Politicians fight like tigers for them, not for us. Politically, we're faintly disreputable, and therefore best ignored. Naturally, we tend to agree with what we're told so often. We tend to think of families as a standard from which we have deviated; their lives are the reality, ours the imitation, the variant, the makeshift. Instead of reshaping our own ways of living, we cobble them together loosely, make do, and, perhaps unconsciously, wait to be rescued from our islands and received into the real world.

Some of us, with independent hearts and good jobs, chose our islands; others were washed ashore on them. We live in a world of departures. Divorce is almost as common as marriage, and lovers get restless and move on. Children write their new addresses in our phone books and go, leaving their beds empty behind them. People die. The retirement plans for two shrivel into plans for one; the hollyhock cottage turns into a more efficient single room. Sometimes, on a rainy day, we seem to have spent our lives losing people we could not bear to lose and go on living, but we do go on. We close the door behind them and hear the tap drip in the sink and the silence pushing against our ears like cotton.

We need to evolve new ways to live, to see ourselves, and to take care of each other. The sheer numbers of us will force some changes, the way group houses and roommates have moved from the campus fringes into the cities and multiplied. Different life plans will have to shoulder themselves forward to stand beside the traditional family values, whatever those are. Maybe the nuclear family will turn out not to be as basic a human arrangement as we've been led to believe; maybe the bonds of friends and tribes and colleagues and kinship groups will turn out to matter too.

We need to cultivate our own serenity, courage, and curiosity, because these go a long way toward a cheerful life. We need to take more chances and more responsibility for action, because it's we who have the time and energy to act; family life may support the soul but it consumes it too. We ought to spend ourselves more freely on challenge, change, risk.

Mostly, though, we need to join hands. Stay in touch. Even when we've fallen freshly in love and the rest of the world's population seems pallid and tedious compared to the one magical human, stay in touch, reaching out through the silvery envelope to make contact with the bread-and-butter others. Remember birthdays. Stay alert for signs of depression in friends; bang on the doors of those retreating into hermitry. Leave cheering messages on their answering machines.

We need to stay open to the simple possibilities of loving. We were told in youth that the whole point and purpose of love, the only possible excuse for it, was to set up a traditional household that becomes a working part of the social machine. Just maybe, though, love comes in other shapes, usable by us, the nontraditional unfamilied legions. Love can show up disguised in various false whiskers, as a runaway nephew, pregnant niece, widowed uncle, cancer victim in the office, AIDS patient down the hall, mad inventor in the next apartment, or someone else's lonely child.

It's possible for us to learn our lessons of self-sufficiency so well we go deaf to loving, or it seems too much of an effort. Rainer Maria Rilke said, "For one human being to love another; that is perhaps the most difficult of all our tasks, the ultimate, the last test and proof, the work for which all other work is but preparation."

Love isn't always ours to call up at will, where it's needed or when we want it, but at least we can leave the door ajar. We can even stay open to sexual love without the remotest possibility of a traditional outcome. Sexual love, as distinct from sex, has taken a terrible beating in the last twenty years and almost vanished from our collective mind under waves of contentiousness, resentment, promiscuity, competition, independence, psychology, anxiety, and pragmatism. It's even lost its name and turned into a meaningful relationship, possibly leading to commitment, which makes it harder to write sonnets about. Still, it was great stuff once, and it's probably still in there waiting if we can chop it loose from all the entangling rubbish.

We must take care not to grow so privately comfortable that we ignore the quiet signals from our fellow humans. Nor should we transfer the sins of the past; those whose husbands ran off with their daughter's best friend, whose wives left town with Ralph from the auto-body shop, should beware of punishing newcomers for the problem. Those whose peerless spouses have died need not keep measuring everyone against their towering shadows. The never-attached should guard against creeping cynicism and generalities. Here, as everywhere, we should stay open to the odd, the unexpected, the unscheduled. It's not so much a lowering of standards as a questioning of their use and purpose, and the various uses of love.

For years, on my quiet street in the city, I could hear the solitary footsteps go by in the dark. Once in the summer, late at night, someone went by alone whistling "Auprès de ma Blonde," and the lilt of it echoed in my mind for weeks. In the winter, the unidentified lone walkers went by coughing; in the spring their coughs were worse. Deeper, like mine.

There are many of us alone here, and more all the time; we all swim in the same river. We aren't on the sidelines, in the backwaters, any more; we've grown to be a solid force in the world and should live accordingly, merry and fruitful, loving and brave. Learn to whistle, and go through our days as full citizens with our thumbs in our pockets, whistling.

For men and women alike, the nuclear family limits enterprise, curtails curiosity, forbids adventure, restricts friendships, and imposes boundaries on all commitments unrelated to itself. Those of us who live alone can make what we please of our days. If we joined hands, what couldn't we accomplish?

There are new cracks in the old system, and changes are being made. More changes will come. It's a sharp creative chisel, this state of unattachment, not always comfortable in the hand but always flexible, for carving our lives into interesting shapes. We need to find new ways to use it well.

ABOUT THE AUTHOR

Following her divorce, Barbara Holland researched this
book by living alone in a wide variety of places and situa-
tions. Currently she finds herself on a mountain in the Virginia Blue Ridge Mountains, companioned by some cats
and assorted wildlife, including an occasional bear. She is
the author of eight books, including *Endangered Pleasures*
and *Mother's Day*.